"This fascinating book is be  ...expected to see in my lifetime on this topic. It is nothing less than an up-to-date survival guide for large women. Its author shows an outstanding grasp of the pitfalls of growing up large, and the remedies and resources that have become available. [One of the] highlights for me [is when she gives a well-deserved nod] to size acceptance pioneer, Kelly Bliss.

"In chapter after chapter, and especially [with] her [journaling prompts] in each chapter, she has great advice, written by someone who has a lifetime of experience in improving her life as a large woman.

"The inclusion of outstanding footnotes throughout the book, as well as lists of resources in the appendices, is worth the price of the book, even if author Glass had written nothing else!"

— Bill Fabrey
Founder, National Association to Advance Fat Acceptance (NAAFA)
and President, Council on Size & Weight Discrimination

Author's Note: *For more information about the history of NAAFA, visit* https://naafa.org/history

"Reading Leslie Glass's book, *Size Matters: The Large Woman's Comprehensive Guide to Living Well* is a gentle and refreshing reminder that all of us—every body—is entitled to a basic set of rights. Glass uses her earlier publication, "The Large Person's Bill of Rights," as a framework for unpacking the myriad ways in which fat people are often denied basic human rights and as an argument for resisting (and even thriving) in a fatphobic culture.

"This book is a wonderfully practical and useful tool for people at every stage of the journey towards body acceptance. In a series of journaling exercises that accompany each chapter, Glass simultaneously challenges readers to hold themselves accountable for their participation in fatphobic culture, while also encouraging a gentle, even liberatory mindset. . . . She challenges readers to inventory and reflect upon their own thoughts about bodies, habits, and emotions surrounding living in bodies that challenge cultural norms.

". . . her work is profoundly personal and written from the perspective of what it's like to be a larger . . . woman who has experienced the pains and joys of living in her body. Her voice joins an important body of work by fat people about fat people. I would enthusiastically share this book with anyone interested in living less fearfully and more joyfully in their bodies."

— Darci Thoune, PhD
Professor, English, University of Wisconsin-La Crosse

SIZE MATTERS

The Large Woman's Comprehensive Guide to Living Well

Leslie C. Glass

Brandylane Publishers, Inc.
Publishing books since 1985

Copyright © 2024 by Leslie C. Glass

No part of this book may be reproduced in any form or by any electronic or mechanical means, or the facilitation thereof, including information storage and retrieval systems, without permission in writing from the publisher, except in the case of brief quotations published in articles and reviews. Any educational institution wishing to photocopy part or all of the work for classroom use, or individual researchers who would like to obtain permission to reprint the work for educational purposes, should contact the publisher.

Cover art by Allison Tunis
www.allisontunisart.com

ISBN: 978-1-958754-58-0
Library of Congress Control Number: 2023922052

Designed by Sami Langston
Project managed by Grace Albritton

Printed in the United States of America

Published by
Brandylane Publishers, Inc.
5 S. 1st Street
Richmond, Virginia 23219

brandylanepublishers.com

For my mother, Jeraldine Moorman Glass.
And for Tamisha Mason (1983-2022), Azhalaun, Tajanae, Penelope, Natalie Claire, and Isabella . . . and for every woman and girl whose experience in their body has and will play a role in shaping the landscape of their lives.

and

A love letter to my ten-year-old self.

CONTENTS

Preface 1
Acknowledgments 9
Chapter One: *Our Experience of our Large Bodies* 11
Chapter Two: *Our Bodies Under Attack* 19
Chapter Three: *Our Bodies in Relationships* 42
Chapter Four: *A Dignified Life* 57
Chapter Five: *Developing Positive Self-Regard* 68
Chapter Six: *Living Fully* 74
Chapter Seven: *Adorning our Large Bodies* 82
Chapter Eight: *Reasonable Accommodations* 90
Chapter Nine: *Making Lifestyle Changes* 95
Chapter Ten: *Managing our Health* 102
Chapter Eleven: *Honoring our Bodies' Limitations* 107
Chapter Twelve: *Taking Up Space* 111
Chapter Thirteen: *Health Care* 117
Conclusion 127
Appendix A 133
Appendix B 135
Appendix C 139
Glossary 143
About the Author 145

PREFACE

> ". . . 'fat' in America was a bad word, heaving with moral judgment like 'stupid' or 'bastard,' and not a mere description like 'short' or 'tall.'"
> — Chimamanda Ngozi Adichie, *Americanah: A Novel*[1]

This book is for every woman who has ever experienced what it is like to live in the world as a large person. I have chosen the word "large" to describe myself and to talk about this subject because many of the other labels that have been applied to people who look like me feel problematic. For example, the word "fat" has been used like a weapon against me and others far too many times in my life to ever feel like I can embrace it. However, I fully respect and appreciate your right to use whatever language resonates with how you feel on the inside and on the outside. I have also struggled with words like "plus-sized" and, especially, "overweight," because they seem to suggest that there is a range of sizes that is *correct? normative? appropriate?* And that anything above that range is not. The word "large" is descriptive and comparative without suggesting that there is a hierarchy that dictates what is normal among the sizes.

In American society, large bodies have been characterized as defective, deficient, and inferior. As a result, those of us who live in large bodies—like most marginalized people—are discriminated against. Recognizing this, in 2015, I wrote *The Large Person's Bill of Rights*.[2] It is a fairly comprehensive[3] response, and call to action, for the ways that the experiences of people who live in large bodies have been devalued. *The Large Person's Bill of Rights* is the basis for everything that is written in this book.

I have been an advocate for size equity since I was in my late teens. Back then, the revolution took place mostly in my mind, as I struggled to transform my relationship with my own body while Americans were simultaneously in the throes of a wave of obsession with thinness and weight loss, the ripples of which are still felt today. I had spent the preceding ten-plus years in the cycle of dieting (Weight Watchers, mostly; before the point system, it was cottage cheese, Melba toast, iceberg lettuce, and TaB—yuck!): losing some weight, then binge eating in an attempt to soothe the excruciating feelings of deprivation; regaining the lost weight, plus ten or so pounds more; back to dieting; and on and on it went. As a teenage girl, my idol was Richard Simmons: I would sit on the floor along with him, cross-legged, desperately trying to absorb the love mantras that he would deliver at the end of his talk show each day—hoping that they would catapult me toward that highly-coveted dream of becoming thin.

It was a trip to Lane Bryant—which, sadly, some thirty years later, is still one of the few brick and mortar retail shops that is exclusively dedicated to selling clothes and accessories for large women—that ultimately shook me out of my hypnosis. The store was promoting a new fashion and lifestyle magazine, called *BBW* (an abbreviation for *Big Beautiful Woman*), for women who were size fourteen and up. It was beautiful and glossy, and the models were well-dressed and sexy. The articles were well written and chock full of positive affirmation. For the first time in my life, I could entertain the possibility that I, like my female family members and friends, like any woman on the street, could be beautiful. And sexy, to boot. It was revolutionary. And, in many ways, remains so. It is still an act of courage for a large woman to move through the world as if we believe that we matter, that we know our value, and that we expect the best that life has to offer. We can expect to be challenged. By the outright bigot who thinks nothing of hurling size-related insults at us. Or the "well-intentioned" friends and family members who don't even think of us as players in the game of life. Or, worst of all, the internalized size bigot: the part of ourselves that has taken in all of the negative messages from society about who we are—that we are unattractive, sloppy, lazy, unintelligent, undisciplined, lacking ambition, unlovable, pitiable, even—**and believes them**.

One of the saddest things that I have ever heard was when Oprah Winfrey once said that despite all of her accomplishments, she would not feel successful until she was able to achieve and maintain her weight loss goals. Wow. Oprah rose from the humblest of beginnings to become an internationally acclaimed talk show host, actor, media mogul, philanthropist, and one of only two Black female billionaires in the world[4] . . . and still, her inability to conform to America's narrowly-defined standard of beauty leaves her feeling like something less than a success. What a loss, that so much of the goodness in her life—and in the lives of all of us who buy into the idea that our value is determined by the size of our bodies—is overshadowed by a nagging, fundamental belief that we are not OK just as we are. If no one has ever told you this before, let me be the first to say it: ***Your worth does not fluctuate with the numbers on the scale.*** Your worth is a constant. It is my great hope that this book will serve as a testament to that idea. And that it will be a companion on your journey toward claiming your birthright: a life that is fulfilling, a life that is lived on your own terms, a life that is lived well.

The Political

There are many books that have been written about wellness as a general theme. This book focuses on the unique challenges that are faced by women with large bodies that can become potential barriers to wellness. As you read this book, you will notice that it focuses a great deal on size as a human rights issue. Why is a book about wellness so focused on social justice? The answer is simple: The discrimination that large people endure, societally and interpersonally, is a major contributing factor to discontent, distress, disorder, and disease. Until we are aware of how these pervasive biases negatively impact our everyday lives, we are missing out on an opportunity to take action to lessen the impact, and to move toward a greater overall sense of wellness.

For my part, I reject the idea that, because we carry a relatively large amount of weight on our bodies—wherever we carry it on our bodies—it is acceptable to treat us as inferior. Doing so is no different than when people are treated poorly because of their gender, race or ethnicity, economic status, religious or spiritual affiliation, gender or sexual orientation, age, or ability. This book introduces the idea that we can experience healing from our awareness of how size-related bias has negatively affected us. And we can use that awareness to transform our relationship with our embodied selves in positive ways. As I am writing this, I am hearing the voices of those who, in recent decades, have risen up—individually and collectively—and taken control of how they would live their lives in the face of oppression: *"I AM WOMAN, HEAR ME ROAR!" "SAY IT LOUD, I'M BLACK AND I'M PROUD!" "¡VIVA LA CAUSA!" "WE'RE HERE, WE'RE QUEER, GET USED TO IT!" "NO JUSTICE, NO PEACE!"*

So . . . what will be our rallying cry?

Size Equity

I refer to my work that promotes the wellness, and the fair and equitable treatment of large people as "size equity" work. How does the term "size equity" differ from terms like "size acceptance"? A size equity perspective is the belief that people who live in large bodies have the same fundamental right—to borrow from the Declaration of Independence—to "Life, Liberty, and the pursuit of Happiness" as anyone else. This is the context from which we are *liberated* to accept our bodies; however, it is important to note that accepting one's body is *still* optional (I will talk more about this in Chapters 1 and 9). A size equity perspective expands the lens and allows for individual differences in how we live and what we believe about our bodies.

About This Book

I decided not to call this book *The Large Woman's "Complete" Guide to Living Well* because I want to leave room for discovering new ideas about what it means to live well. And I am sure that those of you who are reading this book have much to contribute from your own experiences.

I will be using the term "cis-sized" to refer to everyone who is outside of the range of sizes that our society considers large. *"Cis-"* is a Latin prefix that means "on the side of"[5]—in this case, cis-sized people are on the side of what is socially acceptable. This prefix is frequently used to describe people whose gender orientation (identity) is the same as the gender that they were assigned at birth: i.e., cisgender, in contrast to transgender. I am aware that using *"cis-"* in this context is somewhat subjective. Not everyone who might be labeled as cis-sized will perceive themselves as such and, conversely, not everyone who others might think of as large will see themselves that way.

I also want to acknowledge the limitations of my use of the word "woman," and the pronouns "she" and "her," as well as the limitations of my use of the language of monogamy when I talk about romantic relationships. I am aware that this might convey a cisgender female, heteronormative, monogamy-normative tone and focus, and that this might not resonate completely with everyone's experience. I am hoping, however, that anyone who lives in a large body whose identity includes any degree of experience along the female/feminine continuum (including transgender, non-binary, and gender-expansive experiences) will find this book to be useful. As a cisgender woman who wants to stand in solidarity with trans-feminine experiences, I welcome—and am grateful for—any discussions and dialogue that explore where the experiences of large-bodied cis-female and large-bodied trans-feminine folks meet and where they diverge.

How to Use This Book

You, of course, can read this book from cover to cover in one sitting, if you like. However, you will likely get much more out of it if you think of it as a guide on your lifelong journey of living well. In this way, it is not so much a destination that you will reach as it is an ongoing practice. For some of us, this journey will involve healing old emotional wounds. For others of us, it will be about adopting new attitudes. Take as much time as you need (a minute, a day, a week, a month, even years) to absorb, process, and integrate the ideas that you find to be helpful in this book into your life. Some of us might find that working with a coach or a therapist for additional support is helpful. Additionally, the **"Size It Up for Yourself"** exercises that you will find throughout are designed to enhance your understanding and to personalize what you are reading in order to maximize the benefits you may get from this book. I also recommend that you use a journal to explore your own personal experiences around the topics that are addressed in this book.

Content Warnings (CW)

Some of the ideas that are discussed in this book might trigger memories of traumatic experiences that you have had in the past. This could cause you to have an intense emotional response that might feel overwhelming. For some people, this might also include some degree of dissociative experience.[6] I will do my best to add a content warning (CW) at the beginning of any section that I think might create distress for anyone. If you believe that you might feel overwhelmed by reading any part of this book, I recommend that you do one or more of the following things:

- Pace yourself: only read small amounts of the book at a time, and only read as much as feels manageable for you.
- Identify people with whom you can debrief about what you have read and how it made you feel.
- Take some time away from reading the book.
- Skip parts of the book that feel emotionally triggering entirely.
- Seek support from a mental health professional.

FOOTNOTES

1. Adichie, Chimimanda Ngozi. *Americanah: A Novel*. New York: Random House, 2013.

2. Glass, Leslie C. 2015. The Large Person's Bill of Rights. US Copyright #TXu001958704, issued March 18, 2015.

3. In 2017, I added, "I have the right to receive quality health care from health care providers who treat me with dignity and respect, take my symptoms seriously, and engage in thorough assessment and treatment practices that are free from size-related bias" to *The Large Person's Bill of Rights*.

4. Nsehe, Mfonobong, "The Black Billionaires 2017," *Forbes*, March 20, 2017, https://www.forbes.com/sites/mfonobongnsehe/2017/03/20/the-black-billionaires-2017/#152ccc294d6d.

5. Steinmetz, Katy, "This is What 'Cisgender' Means," Living • Language, *Time*, December 23, 2014, http://time.com/3636430/cisgender-definition/

6. Dissociation (or dissociative experience) is a psychological coping response that some people experience when they perceive that there is a threat (danger) present. It involves a felt sense of "being disconnected from the here and now" (Washington State University 2012). A person who is dissociating is not merely daydreaming but is in an altered state of consciousness that can range

from mild to severe. It is an automatic response that typically occurs, to a greater or lesser extent, outside of the person's conscious awareness. A large person might dissociate in an attempt to escape the shame, embarrassment, and humiliation (threat/danger) that comes with being or feeling judged, mistreated, or rejected because of their size. For more information about dissociative experience and dissociative disorders, visit https://depts.washington.edu/hcsats/PDF/TF-%20CBT/pages/7%20Trauma%20Focused%20CBT/Dissociation-Information.pdf

"What is Dissociation and What to Do About It?," University of Washington (website), WA State CBT+2012 https://depts.washington.edu/hcsats/PDF/TF-%20CBT/pages/7%20Trauma%20Focused%20CBT/Dissociation-Information.pdf

ACKNOWLEDGMENTS

With great humility, I give gratitude to that eternal force that I was raised to call God—giving honor and deep respect to the many ways that the people of the world have defined this force for themselves—for the gifts of what feel like an infinite supply of resilience, tenacity, and empathy. They have been, and continue to be, the guiding forces in everything that I do.

I would also like to express my immense gratitude to Janet Sasson Edgette, who saw me before I could see myself. My time with you was a game changer for me, and your loving care resides deep in my bone marrow.

To Carl Julius, my friend of over twenty-five years: much of what I have accomplished in my adult life would not have been possible without your support . . . I am eternally grateful to you, my friend.

Many thanks to my dear Alyssa D'Alconzo Thomas for providing the spark that ignited the flame for me to begin to crystallize my thoughts and experiences around issues related to size equity and size justice. And thank you, Tonya Ladipo, for fanning the flame that set me on the course that led to writing this book.

To the people, throughout my life, who recognized my talent as a writer, and gave me the encouragement and confidence (whether they were aware of it or not) to write, especially: the late Ms. Selma Atkins, my English teacher at Andrew Hamilton Middle School; Deborah Luepnitz,

Ph.D., from the Philadelphia Child Guidance Clinic; and the late Jerry Randolph, Ph.D., at the University of South Carolina School of Social Work.

Thank you to Kelly Bliss of Yoga with Bliss for creating an environment where I can regularly connect with my body in a safe, nurturing, judgment-free space. How fortunate I am to be so intimately connected to the woman that I admired from afar when I used to read your submissions to *BBW* magazine in the late 1980s, and to have discovered—in real life—just how smart and powerful and tender and badass you really are. You have helped me to transform my relationship with my body in ways that I never dreamed that I would.

Thank you, Alison Gerig, LCSW (and my dear, dear friend); Lexx Brown-James, Ph.D., LMFT, CSE; and Andrea Wawrzusin, Ed.D. for holding my hand and holding me accountable as I grappled with some of the more challenging topics in this book.

Lysa Monique Jenkins-Hayden, you were my first (and, maybe, only) model of an American woman who could enjoy food and eating without shame. Your example helped me to liberate myself from a love-hate relationship with food and eating and to embrace them as the profound life pleasure that they are—what a gift! I will always cherish the memory of the years that we functioned as friends/sisters/family for each other.

Joseph C. Yaskin, I am incredibly grateful to have you as a witness and steadfast support on this leg of my journey. Your warmth and positive regard are consistently palpable . . . and make the world feel like a safer and more humane place to exist. Thank you.

To the kind and patient folks at Corner Bakery Café and Iron Hill Brewery (especially Ruth), which became my go-to writing spots for a good bit of the writing of this book: your hospitality is greatly appreciated.

CHAPTER ONE

I HAVE THE RIGHT TO LOVE, ACCEPT, AND APPRECIATE MY BODY, REGARDLESS OF ITS SIZE, SHAPE, CONDITION, OR ABILITY.

> "Not content to bow and bend to the whims of culture / That swoop like vultures / They're eating us away / Eating us away to our extinction."
> — Indigo Girls, "Love's Recovery"[1]

CONTENT WARNING: *This chapter contains the word* ob*se.

It is with great joy and excitement that I invite you on a journey toward wellness. I have spent the better part of the past three years constructing this road map for the journey. It has been custom-crafted to support us—as large women—to take control of our lives, and to feel empowered to take responsibility for our own happiness and well being. How often can we say that our experience has been celebrated? That our needs, wishes, and desires have been the focus of attention? Well, now is the time.

This book will give you the tools that you need to live well. Some of you may have already started on this journey. For those of you who have not, this might be a scary prospect; after years of living in a world that does not value our existence, many of us do not believe that we deserve to live well, or even that it is possible. I want to assure you that it is. Inch by inch . . . step by step . . . leap of faith by leap of faith . . . we are capable of silencing the voices who suggest that we do not deserve to live well. Living well is our fundamental right.

This book is organized around *The Large Person's Bill of Rights*, which is a document that I created as a clear and direct challenge to the ways that we, as large people, have been treated like second-class citizens—by ourselves and by others. Each chapter will focus on one of the thirteen amendments of *The Large Person's Bill of Rights* and will include a discussion of the ways in which our sense of wellness is compromised when we are not living in alignment with the beliefs that are expressed in each amendment. You will also find suggestions for steps that you can take to improve the quality of your life, as well as opportunities to reflect on your own unique experience around the issues that are discussed, by completing the **"Size It Up for Yourself"** exercises.

So . . . shall we get started?

I chose to make this the first amendment of *The Large Person's Bill of Rights* because in many ways, it serves as the foundation for the twelve amendments that follow. It is the development of a loving and accepting attitude toward our bodies that makes it possible for us to believe that we are deserving of the rights that are expressed in each of the subsequent amendments. The idea that a large person could think of their body in positive terms is pretty radical. Except for Santa Claus—who is, himself, merely a mythical character—there are few contexts in American culture where it is acceptable for a person, especially a woman, to have a large body. This leaves those of us who make up the 40% of Americans who the Centers for Disease Control and Prevention label "obese"[2] (such an ugly word) with few opportunities to consume positive information about our bodies. But . . . why are large bodies judged so harshly in our society?

I am reminded of a time, decades ago, that I took my 'tween-aged goddaughter to the Philadelphia Museum of Art. We were leisurely perusing and enjoying the Impressionist paintings when she looked up at me, her cherubic face simultaneously registering confusion and excitement, and exclaimed, "Mom . . . all the women are fat!" I was thrilled that I was given this moment to teach her something positive about her own plump body, after years of witnessing her endure "playful" taunts about it from members of her family of origin. I explained to her that during the time in European history when those paintings were created, it was fashionable—and even desirable—for a woman to be "fat." I later learned that, in many cultures throughout history, large bodies were esteemed because they were seen as a sign of wealth and prosperity—especially during times of famine.[3]

What this tells us is that how we think about our bodies is, to a large extent, dictated by the social and cultural conditions of the time. In recent decades, there has been a feminist argument that suggests that our culture's obsession with weight (and other markers of beauty)—which has been primarily targeted at women—is a mechanism to ensure that men remain in power. If women are constantly preoccupied with what we look like, then we are less likely to seek positions of leadership, power, and authority. In *The Beauty Myth: How Images of Beauty are Used Against Women*, Naomi Wolf refers to dieting as "the most potent political sedative in women's history."[4] American women have spent countless hours, and dollars, restricting our food intake, medicating, pinching, padding, and lacing ourselves into nearly impossible shapes, in pursuit of the "ideal body." Even as we were attempting to achieve the alarmingly tiny wasp waists of the Gilded Age, the narrow hips and flat chests of the Roaring Twenties, the hourglass shape of the Fifties, and the androgynous "heroin chic" of the Nineties, there were always more women who fell outside of the "ideal" than within it. From corsets to teas to intentionally ingesting tapeworms, it is madness when you unpack it all. And a good reason for us to question the beliefs that we hold about the value of one body size (or type) over another. Regardless of the reasons that large bodies have fallen out of favor, and whatever anyone believes about the "appropriateness" of large bodies, at least 40% of us inhabit them. ***And we deserve the same access to a good life as everyone else.***

The Shape of Things

Over the years, as I have continued my own journey toward body like, love, acceptance, and appreciation, I have discovered that when it comes to large bodies, size is one thing . . . and shape is quite another. There appears to be a value hierarchy involving the *shape* of women's bodies as well. For example, I found that most of the images that are meant to be positive, empowering representations of large bodies are of women with waistlines that are much smaller in proportion to their other body dimensions, i.e., the hourglass, the pear shape or, in my cultural context, the "brick house." And who can forget when rapper Sir Mix-a-Lot famously expressed his affinity for women who are "little in the middle, but she got much back?"[5] Consequently, even as I made progress toward loving and accepting my body, I found myself loathing certain parts of it still—my round belly, my flat behind, my narrow hips.

While I was writing this book, I came across a photograph of a large woman in a blog post, with a body shaped like mine, in a confident pose. I was surprised when I realized that I was in love with the image, and that I was in love with the shape of her body. What I learned from that experience was that my appraisal of this woman's body (and its shape) was greatly influenced by the tone of the image. It was a boudoir scene, and she was seated comfortably slouched in a beautiful chair, wearing a floral, midriff-baring poet's blouse and a pair of jeans with the top button tastefully unfastened. She was also wearing cowboy boots, and one of her legs was draped confidently over the arm of the chair. My response was automatic. I felt joy. And I silently committed to no longer settling for jeans that are too big for my legs and behind, making me look like I am wearing a soggy diaper, and to finding a pair that were made to fit *my* body.

Now imagine if the same model was plunked into a different scene. Let's say that she was standing outside of an ice cream shop (no negative stereotype there, right?!) wearing something unflattering (to be clear, I do not believe that a person of any size is obligated to dress in a way that "compliments" their face or body) but still shape-revealing. What if she was slumped over and had a sour expression on her face? How would that affect how I or you might perceive her body? This is how media and advertising work: we are presented with images that are naturally appealing to us and they are paired with the product or service (and, in some cases, the ideology) that is being sold. Like Pavlov's dogs,[6] we eventually learn to associate those pleasant feelings with the product, service, or ideology itself.

Most of the media that I consume continues to showcase one body type—even when the models are super-sized. Those of us whose bodies are further relegated to the sidelines because of their shape do not have to buy into this mythology. We can all celebrate our bodies and feel good about them just as they are. Lately, every time that I wear my favorite Lane Bryant panties—the ones with pink flamingos posing confidently near steel blue palm trees at every couple of inches of white cotton fabric—I consider whether I am shaped like this exquisite bird. After a few weeks of deliberation, I think that I am ready to say—with pride—that I am.

I will talk about issues related to the condition and ability of our large bodies in Chapters 8 – 11 and 13. For now, I invite you to explore your relationship with your own large body by completing this first in a series of "Size It Up for Yourself" exercises:

Size It Up for Yourself:

HOW DO YOU FEEL ABOUT YOUR BODY?

This exercise is designed to help you on your journey toward liking, loving, accepting, and appreciating your body:

Close your eyes (or leave them open if that feels better for you). Now . . . take a slow and gentle breath in through your nose and allow it to travel down to your belly and to linger there for a second or two before gently releasing it up and out through your nose. Repeat this cycle for a few more breaths.

Now, starting from the top of your head, and slowly making your way down to the bottom of your feet, gently place an imaginary sticky flag on any and every part of your body that you already **like, love, accept,** and **appreciate**. Now, open your eyes and record those parts in Table 1. You might also want to write about what it is that you like, love, accept, and appreciate about that part of your body.

Body Part	What I like, love, accept, and appreciate about this part is that:

Table 1

Next, begin the mental inventory again, this time mentally flagging all the parts of your body that you have a negative reaction to. Continue to breathe deeply and gently. This time, as you note these parts (see Table 2, Column A), also note the feelings that come up for you when you think about that part of your body (Column B). If you have any awareness of how these feelings developed, it would be very helpful to write about it in your journal. Note what it would take for you to like, love, accept, and appreciate that part of your body (Column C). For example, would it require a shift in attitude? Or an appreciation for how that part of your body serves you? Or maybe the awareness of someone else's like, love, acceptance, and appreciation of that part of your body?

CHAPTER ONE

Body Part	FEELINGS that come up when I think about this part of my body	What it would take for me to like, love, accept, and appreciate this part of my body

Table 2

Your responses in the second and third columns will determine where you need to focus your attention. For example, if you have a negative reaction to your round belly, and you discover that you have feelings of shame and disgust about your belly, perhaps you decide that what you may need in order to like, love, accept, and appreciate that part of yourself is to understand where these feelings are coming from (by journaling). Your work might be to understand how society's attitudes about round bellies have influenced your feelings about your own belly. From there, you can decide if you want to continue to buy into the idea that the shape of a part of your body is a good reason to dislike it. Hopefully, you will decide that it is not. One way that I developed a greater appreciation for my soft, round belly was when I observed how much my niece, who was less than a year old at the time, enjoyed the feel of it, and how she shamelessly and joyfully hugged and snuggled with it.

I want to clarify something here: if you would like to take steps to alter any part of your body, in any way and for any reason, that is your right (I will talk about this more in Chapter 9). The point here is simply that you can **choose** to examine your negative beliefs about your body and work toward living in it as a loving, accepting, appreciative resident rather than as a hostile, judgmental enemy. Choosing to do so will likely lead you to take better care of your body, to feel safer in it, and to trust it as the vehicle that was meant to support you through your journey in the physical world.

FOOTNOTES

1. "Love's Recovery," CD, track 7 on Indigo Girls, *Indigo Girls*, Epic Records, 1989.
2. "Obesity and Overweight," FastStats Homepage. Centers for Disease Control and Prevention, U.S. Department of Health and Human Services, 2017, https://www.cdc.gov/nchs/fastats/obesity-overweight.htm.
3. "The History of Obesity – The Renaissance to 1910," *Sermo* (blog), July 2, 2015, http://blog.sermo.com/2015/07/02/history-obesity-renaissance-1910/ on 12/2/17.
4. Wolf, Naomi. *The Beauty Myth: How Images of Beauty are Used Against Women.* New York: HarperCollins Publishers Inc., 1991.
5. "Baby Got Back," Sir Mix-a-Lot, *Mack Daddy*, Def American Recordings, Rhyme Cartel Records, 1992.
6. Ivan Pavlov was a Russian scientist who, in the late nineteenth century, began the work of developing the theory of **classical conditioning**. Pavlov paired the ringing of a bell with feeding the dogs in his experiments. Over time, the dogs began to salivate just from the sound of the bell (the salivation response was conditioned)—even when the food was not present.

"Ivan Pavlov and Classical Conditioning: Theory, Experiments & Contributions to Psychology," Study.com, accessed December 12, 2021, https://study.com/academy/lesson/ivan-pavlov-and-classical-conditioning-theory-experiments-contributions-to-psychology.html.

CHAPTER TWO

I HAVE THE RIGHT TO FAIR AND EQUAL TREATMENT, REGARDLESS OF MY SIZE, INCLUDING PROTECTION FROM DISCRIMINATION, RIDICULE, BULLYING, AND HARRASSMENT.

CONTENT WARNING: *This chapter was the hardest of all for me to write. I feel fairly certain that it will be difficult for many of you to read as well. Staring some of these issues squarely in the eye was scary, painful, and emotionally exhausting. I worried about alienating some of you by speaking from a place of raw honesty. My hope is that by starting a conversation around these issues, we can empower ourselves and each other to demand a better quality of life for all of us. If, from the title, you believe that this will be a difficult chapter for you to read, I recommend that you read it last, or after you have read several of the other chapters in the book. I invite you to read it at a pace that feels right for you and that allows time for you to process whatever feelings arise.*
This chapter also contains the words ob*se *and* o*erweight.

I have often said that discrimination against people with large bodies is the last **acceptable** form of prejudice in our society. (Note: In the past few years, this assertion has been challenged by an increase in violence and hateful rhetoric directed toward many historically marginalized groups, as well as by increased attempts to subvert legislation that, in recent decades, has provided protections against discrimination. As I spotlight the injustices that have been suffered by people who live in large bodies, I also want to express my solidarity with other marginalized groups, and to encourage everyone to support and participate in activities that promote the fair and equitable treatment of the recent targets of racist and sexist violence and hate speech: Black, indigenous, and people of color (BIPOC), undocumented immigrants, Asian Americans, trans and queer folks, and women.) Nonetheless, in most places in America today, if someone makes a disparaging remark, or otherwise mistreats someone because of their gender, race or ethnicity, gender or sexual orientation, spiritual or religious beliefs, economic status, age, or ability, there is likely to be at least one person—and often times, many—who will register some sort of protest response: an uncomfortable facial expression, a supportive glance or comment directed to the target and, in some cases, a direct confrontation with the offender. If an individual or a group has committed a hateful act against a member of one of these groups or makes a general statement that suggests that the group is inferior in some way, people band together and rally in support of the group's basic human rights. In recent history, laws have been enacted to protect many marginalized groups from discrimination and persecution.

Not only are people with large bodies less often afforded these kinds of protections, but others are often complicit when incidents of discrimination against, ridicule, bullying, or harassment of large people occur. There are even those who believe that behaviors like "fat-shaming" are justified because it might compel large people to lose weight. Perhaps this belief exists because, somewhere along the line, body size became associated with morality in ways that most other human identifiers (except for gender and sexual orientation) have not. We would never, for example, say that it is right or wrong to be a white person. One just is. This association seems to be made because of the assumption that—just as it has been assumed by many people about gender and sexual orientation—large people can **change** their body size and, therefore, have a **choice** about their circumstances.

To discuss the research around a person's ability to change their body size, or how the cultural ambivalence about food and eating affects how we feel about large bodies, is a distraction from what is most important here. **We ALL deserve to be treated fairly and equitably regardless of our body size.** To understand why we weigh what we weigh is no more necessary for us to be treated fairly and equitably than it is to know why a person's skin is brown.

Discrimination Against Large Bodies

Recent research is providing evidence—and validation—for what many of us already know: large women experience a disproportionate amount of discrimination compared to other marginalized groups. Our identities converge at the intersection of size and gender and, for a percentage of us, race, gender and sexual orientation, religion and spirituality, economic status, age, and ability. Consequently, we are vulnerable to the stigmas and biases that exist for people who are members of those groups as well.

How many of you know who Martha Wash is? I suspect that most of you will draw a blank. OK, now . . . how many of you remember the '90s dance hits "Gonna Make You Sweat (Everybody Dance Now)" and "Strike it Up"? My guess is that (depending on your age) the numbers just increased significantly. Martha Wash is the artist who provided the soulful, life-affirming, blow-the-roof-off-of-the-building vocals that made these songs chart toppers. The reason she is not a household name is because, at the time that these songs were recorded, music videos were at the height of their popularity. The music industry was prioritizing visual compositions and—you guessed it!—Martha Wash is a large woman. Consequently, she was virtually written out of the history of this genre of music. The most infamous (and egregious) examples of how she was ripped off is when the '90s dance groups C+C Music Factory and Black Box duped her into believing that she was recording vocals for another singer's demo.[1] What they did instead was to use a more marketable (translation: thin) singer who lip-synced to Martha's vocals in the video and during some live stage performances, and Martha was either listed as a backing vocalist, or not listed at all, in the albums' liner notes.

The music producers and record label execs seemed to believe that a large body would be so undesirable to audiences that they would not risk using that body—the body that produces the sounds that would make them a lot of money—to promote these songs. Thankfully, that is not where the story ends. Martha went on to sue C+C Music Factory and in doing so, was instrumental in helping to create federal laws that now make giving credit to vocalists mandatory. Yay, Martha! Despite this victory, however, discrimination against large women persists.

Workplace Discrimination

It is a well-documented fact that, currently and historically, women have experienced discrimination in the workplace. For large women, the stereotypes and biases that exist about and against women, in general, are compounded by our society's negative attitudes about large people. For example, although many women face pressure to have an "acceptable" appearance—i.e. to be (and stay) thin and "attractive" at work—large women may be preemptively judged to be unfit for certain roles because of their size. Some companies will not hire large women to greet visitors or to otherwise be "seen," relegating them to spaces where they are practically invisible, because they believe a large woman's presence will negatively affect the company's image. Additionally, several researchers have discovered that large people are perceived as less competent;[2] receive lower starting salaries, are thought of as less qualified, and work longer hours than their cis-sized counterparts.[3] Heavy sigh. As if this is not enough, large people have also been the targets of bullying in the workplace, from sarcastic comments and name-calling all the way to disguised attempts to cause them to lose their jobs.[4] A woman that I know who is super-sized alleges that she was fired from her job as a high school teacher. She said that although she was very popular with the students and that they did well in her class, she was told by the administration that she was fired due to a "performance issue."

Unfortunately, size is currently not a protected category in most state legal systems,[5] which leaves large folks who have been discriminated against with very little legal recourse. I am, however, encouraged by studies out of the University of Connecticut, which found that study participants were predominantly in favor of laws that address discrimination based on weight.[6]

What this suggests to me is that more of us need to start taking legal action when we believe that we are being discriminated against because of our size. By doing so, we can establish stronger legal precedent, which will likely lead to cases getting more attention and being heard more often before judges. This would inevitably lead to changes in employment law that would generate policies requiring employers to be more accountable for making and keeping the workplace safe for their large employees—or face the consequences. We—yes, WE—have the power to change the culture around how people are treated based on their size.

Standing up for ourselves will require a certain amount of boldness. "But *I* am not bold," you say. The hell you're not! You (we) navigate a world that can be unrelentingly cruel to large people every single day and, for better or worse, we get through. We survive, and many of us *thrive*. So, there is no way that I will ever believe that we do not have the fortitude . . . the BOLDNESS . . . to fight for our right to live free from discrimination. Know, too, that we do not have to fight alone. There are formal and informal supports available to us. Check out the Resources section of this book for the contact information for groups who advocate for the fair and equitable treatment of large folks. You might also try contacting human rights advocacy organizations in your area to find out if they can provide support. They might need some education and convincing to think of people's experiences around size as a legitimate issue. You have your own life experience to draw from to help them to understand the pain, suffering, and harm that is caused by being treated unfairly because of your size. I also encourage you to connect with people that you know—especially other large people—for information, support, and co-advocacy.

Ridicule: What's So (F!#@in') Funny?

A colleague and friend who has been an ally in my size equity work asked the question: "why is being fat funny to people?" It is a good question. What is "funny" about a person's body being large, or the ways that we accommodate our size? The closest that I have come to an answer to this question is that when resources are scarce, human beings become competitive. In this case, the resource that has been scarce is the assignment of **unconditional** value to all people. In patriarchal societies, we deem people to be acceptable or unacceptable based on the extent to which they are valued by that society. Traditionally, in American society, women have been valued for their physical appearance and, according to historians, since the mid-nineteenth century, thinness has been the favored condition for women's bodies.[7]

Many of the reasons that historians have identified for the rise in popularity of thinness were means of controlling female bodies and behavior. For example, dietary restrictions to decrease libido and "civil disorder," the fall of the corset, which had been designed to redistribute a woman's flesh so that it was in the form that was the trend at the time (Is your mouth gaping as mine is?), as people began to realize that it was harmful to women's bodies, and the standardization of dress sizes to enable mass production. Women who conformed to these expectations were (and are) rewarded with acceptance and all of the perks that come with being in society's favor. Many women have gone to extremes to maintain, or attempt to acquire, this favor. And no wonder! The costs of not being thought of as "acceptable" are substantial. Large people experience contempt from society simply for existing. This contempt manifests in many ways: social ostracization (leading to isolation) and stigmatization; discrimination, bullying, and harassment; less access to and fewer opportunities for romantic and sexual partnering; and ridicule. Which ultimately amounts to shaming. So, making fun of large people might be a way for some cis-sized individuals to ensure that we continue to feel inferior to them as a means of cementing their more privileged status in society. If this theory is correct, this is most likely happening outside of most people's conscious awareness. That is to say, jockeying for social position is probably deeply embedded in our psyches; even within families, there is an awareness (even if unspoken) of their status in relation to other families in their community and in the world as a whole. Aside from this theory, there are probably also times when all of us unquestioningly model the behaviors of others simply because they are the norm.

How can we feel good about ourselves if we allow others to bully us out of our right to full participation in life? It reminds me of something that one of my professors in my Southern graduate school program told us. He said—to a class of SOCIAL WORK students—that, as an Asian immigrant, he mows his lawn at night to ensure that he does not offend any of his white neighbors. **WHAT?!** What century is this?! If we are to live full and satisfying lives, we cannot hide and shrink into the corners of life to avoid ridicule, and to appease those who are desperately clinging to their own sense of their place in the world.

> ### Size It Up for Yourself – Journal Entry
>
> I invite you to spend some time journaling about the following questions:
> - When you consider the fact that the valuing of one body size over another has been, to a great extent, a means of oppressing women, does that affect how you feel about your own body? If your answer is "yes," how so?
> - How can you use this information to improve your experience in the world? For example, will you find ways to affirm your value **just as you are**?
> - Are there negative assumptions that you make about yourself because of your size that you are now ready to challenge?
> - Have you allowed yourself to be marginalized (pushed to the sidelines) for fear of being made fun of? In what ways? How might you access the courage to claim your place in the world and to live more fully?

Social Media: The Last Outpost

Making fun of large people has also become a common practice on social media. Sadly, there is no shortage of social media posts containing photos or videos (often taken covertly . . . or so the offender believes) of large people doing ordinary, everyday things, like getting out of a car or shopping at Walmart. The captions or memes that are added to these images are intended to make fun of the person being photographed or recorded. I have noticed that some of the same people who would be up in arms if they witnessed discrimination regarding any other aspect of a person's identity on social media are silent when it comes to discrimination based on size.

I think that I understand why this happens: typically, until there is a fairly large segment of society that rejects the mistreatment of a subgroup of society, many individuals are reluctant, if not fearful, to allow their voices of protest to be heard. This has been true for most human rights movements—most recently, perhaps, those that have been organized by the lesbian, gay, bisexual, transgender, and queer (LGBTQ+) communities. I, myself, have been hesitant about calling people out on social media. I have tried to use a gentle approach by simply commenting with a quote from the Reverend Dr. Martin Luther King, Jr.: "Injustice anywhere is a threat to justice everywhere." It has typically not been well-received. I think that I understand this, too: calling someone out publicly likely leads that person to feel embarrassed or ashamed, and no one likes to feel this way. According to author Asam Ahmad, "calling in," which is defined as "speaking privately to an individual who has done some wrong, in order to address the behavior without making a spectacle of the address itself," might be more effective than calling someone out.[8] Each of us has to decide for ourselves if calling someone in or out is the right course of action based on a careful analysis of the costs and benefits involved. Some things to consider are:

- Will the call-out/call-in improve my experience in the world? Think beyond just the visceral satisfaction that you might get from calling the offender to the carpet.
- Could it potentially improve the circumstances of large people, in general?
- Is the offender likely to retaliate in ways that have the potential to cause me harm?

In addition to considering whether to call someone in or out, I suggest that we start to **report** social media posts that are meant to make fun of large people, naming them as instances of hate speech. If enough of us begin to speak out, the tide will shift.

Bullying

Many large people know what it is like to be bullied. It is such a common experience, in fact, that the image that most of us conjure up when we think of a person being bullied is a "fat" kid—second only, perhaps, to the "nerd." Bullies come in all shapes and sizes, exist in every echelon of society, can be any age, and can wreak havoc on a person's life that can last anywhere from the moment that it occurs to the rest of a person's life. Bullies can be in our own families. They can be people that we know personally, or total strangers.

The damage that is done by bullying is immeasurable. It can undermine a person's basic sense of trust in others and feeling of safety in the world. Many people who experience bullying suffer from low self-esteem during, and long after, the bullying has occurred. Children who are bullied are more likely to experience depression and anxiety, health complaints, and a decline in academic performance.[9] For people who are bullied as children who do not receive help and support, these problems can persist, putting them at risk for chronic depression, suicidal thoughts and behavior, anxiety disorders, post-traumatic stress disorder (PTSD), poor health, self-destructive behavior, and substance abuse.[10] Many of them might also have difficulty establishing trusting friendships and relationships. The risks for people whose experience of bullying begins in adulthood are almost identical to the risks for people who experienced bullying as children.[11]

Now that I have reviewed the data related to bullying, I want to take off my social scientist hat to say that, from a human perspective: ***it really hurts.*** It cuts deep. My main bully was a family member. Not only did this person take every opportunity to taunt me about my size when we were children, but they also policed my food choices in ways that created mind-boggling shame for me. Flashback to a family therapy session when I was around fifteen, where this family member, full of rage and indignation, is spewing into the room something like: "There is a carton of orange juice in the refrigerator. Only one person goes into the kitchen. And then the orange juice is GONE! You tell ME who drank it!" Having already become the focal point of my family's dysfunction, I sat there in this circle of mostly adult colluders, smiling nervously, feeling absolutely mortified, defenseless, and unprotected.

There were other random bullies to come. Like the car loaded with college frat-boy types who, when I was in my early twenties, screamed "HARPOON HER!" as I crossed the street. These kinds of experiences become seared into the soul. Regardless of the words or actions of the bully, the message that is internalized by the target is the same: "I don't matter."

WE MATTER.

> ### Size It Up for Yourself – Journal Entry
>
> - Have you ever been teased or bullied about your size?
> - If you have, what **negative beliefs** did you internalize about yourself as a result? You might have to search deep within to uncover them because they may have become such a part of how you see yourself that you might not realize that they were not always there. Once you have located these beliefs, can you remember a time when they were not there? Keep in mind that these might be things that you think about or say to others about yourself with a humorous tone. However, that does not mean that they are not nipping away at your self-esteem and, consequently, your overall sense of wellness.
> - What do you need to recover from the damage that has been done to you by being teased or bullied? Unfortunately, some experiences, no matter how long ago they happened, continue to negatively affect how we feel about ourselves and others. The good news, however, is that we are capable of healing. With information and support, we can activate our internal and external resources to recapture a more positive sense of self.

Cyberbullying

The Internet has created new opportunities for bullying by providing a platform where bullies can arm themselves with anonymity and the knowledge that it is less likely that they will be held accountable for their actions. Cyberbullying is a place where hate thrives. There are two common themes that I have observed in the cyberbullying of large women. And most despicable of all is that they often occur in spaces that large women have created and dedicated to embracing and empowering themselves in an atmosphere of safety.

The first thing that I have noticed is cis-sized bullies invading the space to "inform" everyone—using words like obese and overweight—that being a large person is unhealthy. I have watched as the smart, beautiful, courageous women who created the space to begin with have tried to present scientific and anecdotal evidence that this is not always true. I have witnessed their attempts to fight back by insulting the bully—by almost any means necessary—in response to being insulted. I, personally, have tried to sensitize or educate bullies, which has only served to put them on the defensive. I am convinced, as I believe any reasonable person would be, that these contemptuously delivered "public service announcements" are nothing more than poorly disguised attempts to demean and humiliate large women.

The other theme that I have observed is when bullies level the accusation that size or body positivity is merely an excuse for large people to not address their weight issues. These critiques are loaded with arrogance—as the bully assumes a moral high ground—and loathing. In both instances, the humanity of the intended targets seems to be utterly forgotten. And I hear the pain in the words of the women who respond. I know the pain. Perhaps the best response is to ignore these bullies entirely—to just not feed into their vitriol at all. To adopt a mantra that I learned when I worked in addiction recovery: "Don't let them rent space in your head." These folks can be ignored a lot more easily than a "live," three-dimensional bully can. It is as simple as a page scroll or the click of an "X" to close a page. In cases where the bully's identity is known enough to report them, by all means, DO. The energy that you would expend on confronting them would be much better spent on engaging in life-giving activities, such as connecting with supportive people and resources, raising awareness in your own unique way, and attending to your own self-care needs.

Harassment: The Donut Incident

The first time that I attended a BBW bash (one of a handful of large-scale social events created for large folks that are held throughout the country), during the bash's private pool party, as DJ Jazzy Jeff & The Fresh Prince's "Summa, summa, summa time"[12] joyfully wafted through the air, someone stood on one of the balconies that surrounded the pool at the hotel where the bash was being held and tossed donuts from a bakery box into the pool. Since then, I have wondered: how much hatred must this person be harboring in their heart to take the time to get into their car, drive to a bakery, purchase donuts, and then drive back—all in an attempt to insult and humiliate a group of people who were clearly having a good time, basking in the freedom of being in a non-judgmental space where they could simply be themselves? Equally upsetting was the passive, albeit understandable, response from the group. The donut incident was brought to my attention by a woman who reported on it with the tone of voice of someone who was resigned to these kinds of abuses being an "inevitable" part of her experience. I was livid! And somewhere inside, she must have been, too. However, she seemed to be suffering from a "learned helplessness" of sorts—something that I have observed in others who have been bullied or harassed over long periods of time.

Learned helplessness results when a harmful or unwanted experience occurs repeatedly (in this case, bullying or harassment) and is, or feels, inescapable and unpredictable.[13] After so many of these experiences, which have no fair or just outcome, the person begins to believe (learns) that there is nothing that they can do to escape. They begin to accept the poor treatment without trying to fight back. It is likely that the relative lack of public outcry about the unfair and inequitable treatment of large people contributes to feelings of loneliness, isolation, poor self-esteem, and depression. And unlike members of other marginalized groups, there is a relatively small amount of cohesion, or sense of community, among large folks that we can access for comfort and support.

There are contexts, however, where this is slowly changing. Technology has allowed some size equity activists to create community online, including a number of podcasts that are devoted to this issue (see the Resources section in the back of this book). While this is promising, it will most likely take the coming together of many voices for discrimination, ridicule, bullying, and harassment directed at large people to be seen as unacceptable by society as a whole.

CHAPTER TWO

> ### Size It Up for Yourself – Journal Entry
>
> - What can you, as an individual, do to support the cause of fair and equitable treatment for large people? Remember, it does not have to be a grand gesture—even small acts help to move the cause forward.
> - Can you develop relationships with other large people (or cis-sized allies) that provide support and protection from discrimination, ridicule, bullying, and harassment? It only takes one other person to lessen the feelings of isolation that result from living in a large body in an unfriendly world. Consider looking in the following places for support:
>   - Friends, neighbors, relatives, co-workers, classmates, sorority sisters, members of your religious or spiritual community.
>   - Social media groups.
>   - If you would like, you can start your own mutual support group. For information on how, check out: https://www.wikihow.com/Start-a-Support-Group and https://www.health24.com/Mental-Health/Treatment/Guidelines-on-how-to-start-a-support-group-20120721

In every group that experiences oppression, there are subcategories of oppression that develop *within* the group. Some members may have internalized the negative beliefs, attitudes, and stereotypes that are held by others outside of the group. Individual members of the group will have experienced different degrees of privilege and disadvantage, which can create potential barriers to creating a sense of community and connection. For some, it may be (consciously or otherwise) an attempt to escape the feelings of powerlessness that come with being marginalized. An example of this is when, historically, certain ethnic groups were colonized by Europeans (e.g., African slaves in America, the people of India). The European colonizers introduced beliefs about the inferiority of the colonized peoples' physical attributes, including skin color. Among the colonized, lighter skin gradually became associated with beauty. Being subjugated—and, therefore, rendered powerless—by people with lighter skin led some darker-skinned people to believe that having lighter skin would give them an advantage within colonial systems of oppression. And, in many cases, it did.

The following sections take a closer look at three specific types of intragroup (internal) oppression that occur when large folks seek community with each other.

Internalized Cis-Sized Normativity

As large women, every day we are bombarded by images of women in media that do not look like us. In modern societies, to a great extent, media sets the tone for what is considered "normal." A natural consequence of rarely seeing ourselves represented in the media is that many of us have developed a belief that we are not normal . . . that we are inferior. This belief is reinforced by the direct and indirect feedback that we get from many of the people around us. And so, paradoxically, we learn to guard against feelings of worthlessness and "otherness" by constantly comparing ourselves to the standard that has been set. We believe that there is another, better (thinner) version of ourselves trapped inside our often-despised bodies.

What if we were to begin to think about the media as perpetrating a grand hoax? A couple of years ago, one of my beloved cis-sized clients was struggling with feeling unattractive. I gave her a homework assignment for the walk home: As you walk down the street (my office is in a major metropolitan area), count the number of people that you see who look like what our society considers to be "beautiful." The next time that we met, she reported—with great astonishment—that, on her mile-long walk (where she probably passed a couple of hundred people), she had barely seen anyone who fit the bill! This impromptu social experiment was powerful. The takeaway: we can choose to stay chained to the idea that our bodies need to conform to society's unrealistic, oppressive standard of beauty and acceptability . . . or we can walk boldly in the knowledge that what the body positivity movement is saying is the unfiltered truth: **ALL BODIES ARE GOOD BODIES.** Radical, huh?

The belief in cis-sized normativity shows up in many ways in the everyday lives of large women. Many of these will be explored in more depth throughout this book. For now, let's take some time to think about the ways that we unintentionally reinforce the idea of cis-sized normativity.

Size It Up for Yourself – Journal Entry

It might be easier to do this if we ask ourselves these two questions:

(a) What are the everyday situations that I find myself in where I believe that my size is a barrier in some way?

(b) In these situations, do I believe that it is my body that needs to change, or do I allow for the possibility that there might be—or, in some cases, needs to be—a way to make a change in the circumstance?

Here are two examples:

(a) When I observe cis-sized people fitting easily into a booth at a restaurant, do I believe that I need to lose weight in order to fit into the booths of the world comfortably? Or do I consider the possibility that it is the restaurant owner's responsibility to have accessible seating available for ***everyone***? After all, if they are willing to take our money, shouldn't they be willing to take reasonable measures to ensure that our dining experience is pleasant?

(b) A harder to recognize example to consider is this: At an extended family gathering, the cis-sized single women are asked about their romantic lives (e.g., "are you seeing anyone?") while I, as a large woman, am not. Do I recognize the potential assumption that I do not have a partner or, in some cases, might not even be interested in having a partner, as cis-sized normativity at work? These thoughts might not come into your conscious awareness; however, your body might be signaling you (e.g., with a pit in your stomach, a lump in your throat, a tightening of your muscles) that there is an injustice occurring in the moment.

Are there experiences that you believe are only available to cis-sized people? Opportunities for dating and partnering, for example, or even having a positive sense of self? What behaviors, activities, or experiences are reinforcing these assumptions for you? Here are some common ones:

- Over-consuming media that shows only or mostly images of cis-sized people.
- Avoiding or not participating in activities that you deem "not for large people."

> ### Size It Up for Yourself – Journal Entry
>
> *(continued)*
> - Not asking for reasonable accommodations when you need them. (I am aware that this is much easier said than done, so please don't judge yourself if you do not. I will be talking about this more in Chapter 8.)
> - Always deferring to the wishes, preferences, and opinions of cis-sized friends, family members, co-workers, classmates, etc.
> - Not thinking of yourself as a suitable dating partner.
> - Fading into the background when you are the only large person who is present in social situations.
>
> What can you do to "normalize" your own experiences? For example, I have recently been practicing being unapologetic and unashamed about taking the time that I need to get up from seating. In the past, I have always felt the need to get up as quickly as I can and to show no signs of struggle. Reflecting on this now, it feels unintentionally invalidating of my own experience in the world. It is an attempt to be "normal," because "normal," fully able-bodied, cis-sized people do not struggle to get up from their chairs.

Sizeism

Sizeism occurs whenever there is a negative bias expressed, through words, beliefs, or actions, about human body size (weight). When large women hold sizeist beliefs about other large women, it in some ways represents the flip side of the coin from internalized cis-sized normativity. They are both a product of the attempts that we make to feel good about ourselves in a world that is constantly telling us that we have no value. These beliefs are commonly expressed when large women either (a) respond negatively to women who are larger than they are; or (b) judge women who are not as large as they are to be outsiders to the size acceptance movement.

When we respond negatively to women who are larger than we are, our responses are sometimes silent, internal judgments. At other times, they might be whispers among "friends," or parts of later conversations with others, as in, "I saw a woman today who was SO big." It is scary for me—as someone who is asking you to believe in the goodness of your large body—to admit that I have been guilty of judging other large women's bodies as well. I want to take a moment to ask for forgiveness from myself, and from every other large woman on the planet. For my entire life, I, like most of you, have been spoon-fed the idea that, if a woman's body is not at or below a certain size, then her value and worth decrease significantly. There was a time when I certainly believed this about myself. It has been a journey to arrive at this point in my life—where I believe in the inherent beauty and value of ALL bodies. So, my confession feels important. It allows me to say this with authenticity: as long as we judge other women's bodies, we are not free to develop a kind and loving relationship with our own bodies.

There are also people who participate in the size acceptance community who do not believe that women who fall *below* a certain size belong in the movement or in large body-affirming spaces. I took a sampling of the perspectives of women across the spectrum of large, as well as what some size equity advocates have to say on the subject. In response to the prevalence of this kind of "gatekeeping" in online spaces, Linda, author of the blog "Fluffy Kitten Party," created several exceptional graphics that delineate and approximate a spectrum of the most commonly used categories of "fat".[14] M. Ferguson, creator of the "Fat Positive Cooperative," a web site for fat-positive resources and community-building, talks about the correlation between "levels" of fatness (i.e., size) and levels of social privilege;[15] she and other writers, like Caleb Luna, who speaks out against "superfat erasure," recognize that being smaller is associated with having more privilege.[16] As someone who is at the lower end of the spectrum, I can say that I have been mistreated, excluded, and marginalized because of my size enough in my life that it has left me with wound upon wound upon wound. And I have had the experience of profound loneliness as a large person in a world that favors cis-sized bodies. Like blogger Marie Southard Ospina,[17] I have arrived at the conclusion that this is a case that involves the "both-and": it is **both** true that women who are at the higher end of the spectrum of large bodies (and, therefore, the most marginalized) should have their experiences be at the center of the movement; **and** that women who are at the lower end of the spectrum should have their experiences validated, even as we recognize our privilege, and everything that comes with it, in being seen as more acceptable by society. This movement is for all of us who have been oppressed because of the size of our bodies. As I benefit from the support of participating in size-affirming communities, I hope that I am an ally to people at the higher end of the spectrum, and I maintain an openness to having my implicit biases challenged. As M. Ferguson asserts:

> Fatphobic society would have us fat folk lean into these definitions as a hierarchy that pits small fats against mid-fats and superfats, but doing so harms everyone, fat or not. **We can defy this hierarchy by prioritizing the voices and lived experience of superfats and by checking the privilege of small fats and mid-fats.**

Your pain and suffering are legitimate.
My pain and suffering are legitimate.
Her pain and suffering are legitimate.

Size It Up for Yourself – Journal Entry

- Are there ways that you judge other large women?
- Are there negative stereotypes about large people that you believe about yourself and other large folks? For example, I have heard some large folks "joke" about how much they like to eat—in some cases, even saying in an exaggerated, matter-of-fact tone, "I'm greedy." I believe that this is often (if not always) a defensive posture—a pre-emptive attempt to take the sting out of the possibility that other people might be thinking the same thing about them. So, let's honor this as a coping strategy, with the gentle reminder that, while it might be effective in the moment, it likely causes harm in the long run: a negative (inaccurate) belief about large people is reinforced; and this person has just made another "deposit" into their poor self-esteem jar.
- How can you be more mindful about how your behavior might be negatively affecting how you feel about yourself and other large folks?
- What can you do to support the idea that size-affirming spaces should be welcoming and inclusive?

Intersectionality

The term **intersectionality** was first articulated by Columbia University Law professor Kimberlé Crenshaw and was used to describe the experience of Black women who found that their participation in the feminist and anti-racism movements was overshadowed by bias against them within each group.[18] They experienced discrimination from white feminists for being Black, and they experienced discrimination from men in anti-racism groups for being women. Sadly, this appears to happen when large folks organize for fellowship and support as well. And just as when I am confronted with a situation that I think involves racial bias in the world, I find myself questioning my instincts when I feel like I am being treated differently because of my race in some size-affirming spaces that are predominantly white.

I always enter these spaces with an open heart, and with the expectation that everyone else is going to be as excited to see me—a fellow traveler on this treacherous, lonely road—as I am to see them. When this does not happen, I instinctively search for clues as to why. After I rule out other factors—being a first-timer at a particular event (often referred to as being a "newbie"); intracommunity sizeism; even that my height might be intimidating to some—I am prone to attributing some people's lack of warmth towards me to my being Black. And, more specifically, my being a Black woman. Black men are often treated like superstars at these events and are immensely desired as romantic and hook-up partners.

Before we start celebrating this as progress toward racial equality, I should note that there is evidence that some white women who live in large bodies believe that Black men will be more likely to date, marry, and have sex with them than white men will because large female bodies are more accepted in the Black community. This is not as true for Black men who have upward social mobility because they are more likely to adopt Eurocentric values. In addition, some white women in size-affirming spaces have confirmed with me directly (and enthusiastically) that the slavery-era stereotype about Black men having large penises is still around. For anyone who might think of this as a compliment, it was likely one of many myths that served to further dehumanize and exoticize Black men and women.

There is a small but growing and powerful part of me that *does* trust my instincts around matters of race. After all, I have had fifty-six years of experience as a Black person in America. And even when I am wrong, I expect a certain amount of grace. As Hicks alludes to in her article, "Dear White Folks: Black People are Sensitive to Race," after a lifetime of experiencing racial microaggressions, Black folks have earned our sensitivity about race.[19]

Of course, race is not the only part of some people's identities that intersects with their identity as a large person. In some size-affirming spaces, I have also observed large men being banished to the margin. Many of the large women who are present in these spaces appear to undervalue the few large men who are there as potential dating partners. These men are often treated as non-sexual beings who are mostly suited to be fun and friendly platonic friends and allies. I should say that I have only attended social events; the landscape might be quite different in spaces where people gather for advocacy and other forms of support. I also saw more inclusion and appreciation of large men when I attended bashes that were hosted by large men. We can probably attribute this undervaluing to the same internalized cis-sized normativity and internalized sizeism that is discussed above. For example, I have heard quite a few large women say that they are not attracted to large men. And I have witnessed large women pursuing cis-sized men as if acquiring their attention is a badge of honor.

To some extent, LGBTQ+ identities have also been marginalized although, perhaps, less so than in the general population. For example, while the size-affirming spaces that I know of have not specifically put out calls welcoming LGBTQ+ folks to attend events, when they are present, they appear to be welcomed and accepted as part of the community. The basis of the marginalization that I see is in how the advertising for some of the events is worded in a way that is cis- and heteronormative. On the other hand, there appears to be widespread acceptance of polyamorous and kink-inclusive relationships in size-affirming spaces. Whatever love exists between the two communities, however, does not appear to be mutual. In her 2013 article, "Sized Up: Why Fat is a Queer and Feminist Issue," Mollow articulates what anyone who has spent time in many LGBTQ+ spaces already knows: the community as a whole values thinness much like mainstream America does, and is deeply entrenched in a politically-motivated, fear-driven war on fat.[20] She gives a compelling argument that questions whether large bodies are the latest "scapegoat" for an American consciousness that seems to need a "disempowered 'other'." There are some subgroups within the LGBTQ+ community that advocate for the inclusion and affirmation of large bodies (see the Resources section of this book for a listing of some of them); however, they continue to exist on the fringe of the community at large.

As I mentioned earlier in this chapter, the one essential characteristic that large people, as a group, do not have that other groups have is **cohesion**—there is not a unifying, "felt sense" that we, as individuals, are part of a group. According to "Management Notes," a blog that provides information for leaders of organizations and groups, two of the basic characteristics of groups are (a) that members of the group interact and are interdependent and (b) that they share a collective identity.[21] These attributes are grievously missing among large people as a collective body. There are relatively few examples of solidarity, or a sense of belonging to a group. I sometimes joke with family members and friends about the fact that whenever I am in a situation where the majority of the people who are there are white, if there is another Black person present, we ALWAYS make eye contact and acknowledge each other in some subtle way. In that brief exchange, there is so much that is being communicated: an acknowledgment of our shared history and culture; our awareness that there is a chance that we are in hostile territory; the comfort of knowing that there is a level of safety between us. It is, in fact, those brief exchanges that make an often-unsafe world feel more manageable. Imagine if this kind of expression of kinship were available to large people. How much better would it feel to be in the world? How much more empowered would we feel?

> ### Size It Up for Yourself – Journal Entry
>
> If you are part of the power-holding race, gender, or gender or sexual orientation in a size-affirming space, what can you personally do to ensure that others feel welcome and included? If you are a leader in the community, how can you use your influence to make size-affirming spaces feel safe for everyone?

FOOTNOTES

1. Newman, Jason, "Martha Wash: The Most Famous Unknown Singer of the '90s Speaks Out," *Rolling Stone*, September 2, 2014, https://www.rollingstone.com/music/music-news/martha-wash-the-most-famousunknown-singer-of-the-90s-speaks-out-231182/.

2. Levine, E. E. and Schweitzer, M. E., "The Affective and Interpersonal Consequences of Obesity," *Organizational Behavior and Human Decision Processes* 127, (2015): 66-84, https://repository.upenn.edu/fnc_papers/87/ doi/10.1016/j.obhdp.2015.01.002.

3. Schulte, P. A., Wagner, G. R., Ostry, A., Blanciforti, L. A., Cutlip, R. G., Krajnak, K. M., Luster, M., Munson, A. E., O'Callaghan, J. P., Parks. C. G., Simeonova, P. P. and Miller, D. B., "Work, Obesity, and Occupational Safety and Health, *American Journal of Public Health* 97, no. 3, (March 2007): 428 – 436, https://www.ncbi.nlm.nih.gov/PMC1805035.

4. van der Zee, Renata, "Demoted or Dismissed Because of Your Weight? The Reality of the Size Ceiling," *The Guardian*, August 30,2017, https://www.theguardian.com/inequality/2017/aug/30/demoted-dismissed-weight-size-ceiling-work-discrimination.

5. Martin, Areva "49 States Legally Allow Employers to Discriminate Based on Weight," *Time*, Motto, Time USA, LLC, August 16, 2017, https://time.com/4883176/weight-discrimination-workplace-laws/.

Puhl, Rebecca M., "Weight Discrimination is Rampant. Yet in Most Places It's Still Legal," *The Washington Post*, June 21, 2019, https://www.washingtonpost.com/outlook/weight-discrimination-is-rampant-yet-in-most-places-its-stilllegal/2019/06/21/f958613e-9394-11e9-b72d-d56510fa753e_story.html. Currently, Michigan is the only state that legally prohibits discrimination based on weight (Martin 2017), as articulated in the Elliott-Larsen Civil Rights Act of 1976 (Act 453). Go to https://www.michigan.gov/documents/act_453_elliott_larsen_8772_7.pdf to read the entire act. Some cities, however, like San Francisco and Binghamton, NY, have passed legislation prohibiting discrimination based on weight.

6. Puhl, R. M., Suh, Y., and Li, X., "Legislating for Weight-Based Equality: National Trends in Public Support for Laws to Prohibit Weight Discrimination," London: International Journal of Obesity 40, no. 8, (August 2016): 1320 – 4, https://www.ncbi.nlm.nih.gov/pubmed/27089997

7. Natalie Wolchover, "The Real Skinny: Experts Trace America's Thin Obsession." Live Science. Future US, Inc., published on January 26, 2012. https://www.livescience.com/18131-women-thin-dieting-history.html.

8. Ahmad, Asam, "A Note on Call-Out Culture," Briarpatch Magazine (blog), March 2, 2015, https://briarpatchmagazine.com/articles/view/a-note-on-call-out-culture.

9. "Effects of Bullying," stopbullying.gov, U.S. Department of Health and Human Services, last reviewed May 21, 2021, https://www.stopbullying.gov/at-risk/effects/index.

10. Hurley, Katie. "Short Term and Long Term Effects of Bullying." Psy-

com. Updated September 26, 2018. https://www.psycom.net/effects-of-bullying#longtermeffects-victim-.

11. Colino, Stacey, "The Long Reach of Adult Bullying," Home/Wellness/Mind, U.S. News & World Report, December 15, 2017, https://health.usnews.com/wellness/mind/articles/2017-12-15/how-adult-bullying-impacts-your-mental-and-physical-heath.

12. "Summertime," DJ Jazzy Jeff & The Fresh Prince, Homebase, Jive, 1991.

13.. Maier, Steven F. and Seligman, Martin E., "Learned Helplessness: Theory and Evidence," Journal of Experimental Psychology: General 105, no. 1 (1976): 3-46, https://psycnet.apa.org/doi/10.1037/0096-3445.105.1.3.

14. Linda, "Fategories — Understanding 'Smallfat Fragility' & the Fat Spectrum," Fluffy Kitten Party (blog), October 5, 2019. https://fluffykittenparty.com/2019/10/05/fategories-understanding-smallfat-fragility-the-fat-spectrum/.

15.. Ferguson, M., "Exact Numbers and Levels of Fatness," Fat Positive Cooperative, WordPress.com, January 3, 2019, https://fatpositivecooperative.com/2019/01/03/exact-numbers-and-levels-of-fatness/.

16. Luna, Caleb, "Superfat Erasure: 4 Ways Smaller Fat Bodies Crowd the Conversation," The Body is Not an Apology, April 19, 2019, https://thebodyisnotanapology.com/magazine/super-fat-erasure-how-smaller-fat-bodies-crowd-the-conversation/.

17. Ospina, Marie Southard, "The "Small Fat" Complex in Body Positivity & Why It's Not Entirely Justified," Fashion, Bustle, November 24, 2015, https://www.bustle.com/articles/125803-the-small-fat-complex-in-body-positivity-why-its-not-entirely-justified.

18. Crenshaw, Kimberlé, "Why Intersectionality Can't Wait," In Theory, The Washington Post, September 24, 2015, https://www.washingtonpost.com/news/in-theory/wp/2015/09/24/why-intersectionality-cant-wait/?noredirect=on&utm_term=.d9ee468e7ce3.

"Kimberlé Crenshaw on Intersectionality, More Than Two Decades Later," Stories and News, Columbia Law School, The Trustees of Columbia University in the City of New York, October 12, 2018, https://www.law.columbia.edu/pt-br/news/2017/06/kimberle-crenshaw-intersectionality.

19. Hicks, Joyce Clark, "Dear White Folks: Black People are Sensitive to Race," Ebony.com, March 26, 2012, https://www.ebony.com/news/dear-white-folks-black-people-are-sensitive-to-race-so-and-what/.

20. Mollow, Anna, "Sized Up: Why Fat is a Queer and Feminist Issue," BitchMedia, May 10, 2013 https://bitchmedia.org/article/sized-up-fat-feminist-queer-disability.

21. "Characteristics of Group – What is a group? | Organizational Behavior," Management Notes, September 11, 2016, https://www.managementnote.com/featurescharacteristics-group-group-organizational-behaviour/.

CHAPTER THREE

I HAVE THE RIGHT TO BE LIKED, LOVED, CARED FOR, AND APPRECIATED BY OTHERS, REGARDLESS OF MY SIZE.

Sounds obvious, right? But for many of us who live in large bodies, the experience of enduring constant negative messages about our bodies leaves us doubting, or completely not believing, the truth of this amendment. These negative messages come from many sources: being bullied and ridiculed as children and adults (see Chapter 2); having family members express disapproval about our size; having a harder time finding romantic partners or being mistreated or undervalued by them; being excluded from social groups (e.g., friendship groups, sports teams); and diet culture, to name a few. It is possible, however, to reclaim and rediscover our sense of our own value and worth.

Creating Community: The Importance of Relationships

I cannot emphasize this strongly enough: **loving, supportive relationships are essential to our sense of well-being.** Contrary to popular belief, our sense of ourselves as valuable individuals does not develop in a vacuum. We cannot simply will ourselves to self-acceptance, and we won't get there by reciting affirmations in the mirror. Relationships are the source from which positive self-esteem flows—starting from our earliest relationships with our parent(s) and/or primary caregiver(s), and later shifting to our peers and other social groups.[1] How much we like, love, care about, and appreciate ourselves is largely influenced by the quality of those relationships. If we receive approving, encouraging feedback, we internalize good feelings about ourselves. On the other hand, if we are met with criticism, judgment, rejection, or a lack of interest, we learn to feel badly about ourselves.

Think about what this means for those of us who have experienced size-related criticism for all, or even part, of our lives. We are likely to struggle significantly with feelings of low self-worth. One of the most important things that we can do for ourselves is to develop and nurture relationships with people who we can trust, who are kind to us, and who provide us with positive support. I know this is easier said than done. And the older we get, the fewer everyday opportunities to make new friends (like school or work) are available to us. So, we might have to work a little harder to find new relationships.

If you are fortunate enough to already have strong, supportive, dependable relationships, that is wonderful. However, if you do not, don't despair! There are lots of ways that you can begin to develop new relationships and enhance existing ones. A framework that I have developed and have found to be helpful for many of my clients is to think about relationships in terms of **level** of relationship. What this means is that not every relationship that you have has to meet all your relational needs. I love to use the example of one of my friends, who I will call T. T is a former co-worker whom I adore. From my first encounters with her, however, I became aware that she did not seem comfortable dealing with difficult emotions. In team meetings, she would be the first staff member to inject humor into the conversations about our clients, who were dealing with some pretty heavy issues: homelessness, intimate partner violence, losing parental rights to their children, you name it. I don't think that I ever realized, until this moment, how important T's jokes and laughter were to the work that we were doing. It was HEAVY. She was the case manager who coordinated resources for the women and children in the program, and she was deeply committed to that work. But she brought an aura of lightness, helping us to not take ourselves and our work too seriously.

During our time at the agency, T and I would occasionally go out for dinner or happy hour, or just hang out after work. We have continued that relationship. There are no expectations about how often we will see each other. That we will show up for each other during difficult times—or celebratory ones, for that matter. T is not the person to seek out if I need support around processing a complicated or deeply emotional experience. However, T is one of the only people in my life who will call me on a whim and invite me to a *Purple Rain* Sing-Along! She is a source of brightness and fun in my life. Of course, we need more than just fun from our relationships. And that is where the idea of levels comes in. Different relationships can meet different relational needs. This is a useful way of thinking whether we are talking about existing relationships or relationships that are yet to be formed.

Size It Up for Yourself – Journal Entry

Part I: Assessing your relationship needs

What do you need from the people in your life? Some examples of what you might need are: opportunities for fun; companionship; emotional support; general support (e.g., an occasional babysitter, a study partner, etc.); a sense of family (see my discussion of chosen family relationships later in this chapter); etc. If it is helpful, you can make a grid with a column (or row) for each need that you have.

Who are the people in your life who currently meet these needs? In some cases, the answer might be "no one." Plug anyone who comes to mind beneath (column) or beside (row) the corresponding need on your grid.

What needs do you have that could be being met by someone in your life if you were to allow them to or ask them to? Plug those folks into your grid under the corresponding need.

Who in your life are you expecting to meet certain needs that they are unwilling or incapable of meeting? This last question can be a difficult one to come to terms with. If you find yourself in this situation with someone, try not to take it personally. Their inability or unwillingness to meet certain needs of yours probably has more to do with their own life and experiences than it does with you, or even how they feel about you. Whatever the reason, you are better off looking to other relationships to have those needs met rather than setting yourself up for chronic disappointment. Besides, when we hold on to expectations of others that are repeatedly shattered, we are unintentionally reinforcing the idea that we are not worthy of other people's positive regard, love, care, and appreciation.

A final note: please also be aware that there are some needs that we are responsible for meeting for ourselves. For example, depending on the norms of our society and our specific cultural beliefs, we might be responsible for meeting our own basic survival needs.

Size It Up for Yourself – Journal Entry

Part II: Taking action
Where can you meet new people? Here are some ideas:
- **Find things that you love, like, or have an interest in doing.** This will create organic opportunities to connect with others, and you are likely to meet people who share your interests while doing something that you enjoy.
- **Start or join a Meetup group (www.Meetup.com).** Meetup.com is one way that technology has knocked it out of the park in helping people to stay connected and engaged in meaningful social activity. It is an Internet platform that is based on a simple idea: regular folks post an idea for a group activity that they would like to participate in. Other regular folks express an interest in the group. Plans are made to meet up. The sky is the limit when it comes to the kind of meetup groups that can be posted.
- **Get involved with groups and organizations that promote size equity.** Every day, people are organizing and gathering in the spirit of supporting, advocating for, and celebrating people who live in large bodies. Check out the Resources section of this book for a list of some of these groups and organizations. Facebook is also a good resource.
- **Volunteer**
- **Attend one of the BBW parties (bashes) that are held throughout the country.** For a list of the bashes that are known to this author, see the Resources section of this book.
- For those of you who believe that you might benefit from one, some therapists offer **Social Skills Training** groups and workshops (sometimes called **Interpersonal Process groups**). These groups provide an opportunity to learn, or improve, social skills by interacting with other group members in a safe and supportive space and by practicing new behaviors in real time.

After the Bash

As I mentioned in the preceding journal exercise, one of the more popular ways that large folks have created community is by hosting grand-scale social events that are known as bashes. A bash is typically a multi-day event where people come to gather for fellowship and fun. Some bashes consist only of several consecutive nights of partying, going well into the early morning hours; others also include daytime activities, such as games, sports, vendor fairs, fashion shows, pool parties, workshops, excursions, and other forms of entertainment and recreation. I have been attending bashes since 2007. They are the one space on the planet where I feel completely—resplendently—like myself, in my body, without any thoughts or feelings of self-consciousness. They are a temporary utopia where I can inhale and exhale deeply and walk in the fullness of who I am. I feel weightless, as if I am orbiting through time and space precisely as the person that I was meant to be.

These feelings come from knowing that mostly everyone in attendance knows what it is like to be a large person in a world that is unkind and rejecting of large bodies. These feelings aside, however, the bashes that I have attended thus far do not seem to have evolved to the point where they are consistently safe, nurturing spaces for large women. In my experience, lurking within the apparent goodwill were several negative dynamics. Some women formed cliques, which they used to exclude and make hateful and derogatory comments about other women who were in attendance; the comments were mostly size-related comparisons and judgments about some women's sexual behavior. I saw predatory men whose only purpose for being there seemed to be to exploit women who were suffering from feelings of low self-worth, using them for sex, free meals, and free lodging. And then there were the handful of men who fetishize large women: who stood on the sidelines, drinks in hand, like vultures ready to pounce. These dynamics undermined the safety of a space that was, theoretically, intended to empower.

There was often no programming that focused on topics of interest and concern to the large community, and the promoters themselves sometimes seemed to be simply taking advantage of a money-making opportunity. One of the largest bashes in the country is held, annually, at an old, dirty, dilapidated hotel. Think about what this likely means for the collective morale of the community. This hotel *itself* suffers from low self-esteem. From the moment that I walked through the door, I felt deflated. I was expecting to be greeted with immediate relief from the 95° desert temperature that my East Coast body was not accustomed to, but the air conditioning was barely working. I looked around for a chair to collapse into and everything in the lobby—especially the furniture—was filthy! And that was only my introduction to the hotel; I could write a paragraph about the plumbing problems that we encountered. I also heard the rumblings of some folks who have accessibility concerns on the elevator and in public spaces. In no way was this hotel suitable for large bodies: from the long distance from the lobby to the guest rooms to the tiny bathrooms with doors that opened inward, leaving little room for a large body to maneuver around.

There are exceptions. Until recently, the National Association to Advance Fat Acceptance (NAAFA) held an annual conference that focused on advocacy, education, and support. There were parties at this conference, to be sure, but they were not the main event. I also know of a few couples who met at BBW events who are enjoying long-term partnerships, and some positive, lasting friendships have developed out of connections that were made at these events. The bashes that I have attended on the East Coast have been held at hotels outside of major metropolitan areas, which might make it more cost-effective for party promoters to choose nicer hotels.

But what happens after the bash? When the music stops and the alcohol is no longer flowing, is it time to check in with yourself? The constant thump from the DJ booth, heavy alcohol consumption, and the complicated social dynamics can combine to have a numbing or freezing effect on our feelings, overwhelming our emotional circuitry. Consider doing a mental rewind for a post-bash wellness check.

CHAPTER THREE

Size It Up for Yourself – Post Bash Wellness Check

Did you come to the bash with certain expectations for what would happen there? Were your expectations met? Using my own experience as an example, I am wondering if you had some of these expectations:

- Programming that would help you to feel good about yourself and improve your experience in the world.
- Making new friends.
- Meeting someone and developing a romantic relationship.
- _____

What, if anything, do you need now to restore your pre-bash sense of wellness?

- More sleep and rest?
- To limit your alcohol consumption?
- To get back on track with your health-sustaining medications (including vitamins and supplements)?
- To connect with people who are loving, supportive, and affirming?
- To do things that make you feel good about yourself?
- To access media (books and magazines; movies and television shows; websites and blogs) with positive images and stories about large people (see the Resources section of this book for some suggestions)?

What can you take away from the experience to improve how you feel about yourself, and to set the bar for future experiences?

Were you affected by any of the negative dynamics that I have observed at bashes?

- Cliques that felt exclusionary and rejecting?
- The presence of predatory men who seem to devalue, objectify, exploit, and sometimes fetishize large women?
- Unwanted touch from men and/or women?
- _____

How can you avoid, or respond differently, to these experiences in the future?

Another thing that commonly occurs after a bash may take you by surprise, but it deserves your attention. And it is a result of the *positive* experiences at bashes. Many people experience a temporary mild depression as they return to their everyday life. This feeling might be present whether we are aware of it or not, and it is likely the result of re-entering spaces that are not as accepting—or even harshly rejecting and critical—of large bodies. We might find it difficult to resume our normal routine. Or we might feel a lack of enthusiasm or motivation around things like work and social engagements. Some people might feel let down because they did not (or did!) connect with someone romantically or sexually at the bash and believe that there will be no opportunities for this in the cis-sized (only)-affirming world. If depression is a familiar part of your experience, you might experience the post-bash blues more intensely.

For me, this phenomenon naturally points to the need for more size-friendly/size-affirming spaces and experiences in everyday life. Folks should not have to wait for one week(end) out of the year to feel good about themselves! On a large scale, we, as a community, need to be more active about raising awareness, changing attitudes, and lobbying for changes in laws and policies that do not factor in the needs of people of size. In the meantime, **how can you incorporate more size-affirming experiences into your life?** Be sure to consult the Resources section of this book for ideas and opportunities.

Family Relationships

Some of us have been able to get a good deal of our relational needs met by our families. Whether they are our biological, adoptive, or foster families, or spontaneously created kinship networks, they have provided us with the love and care we need to develop a healthy sense of self. If this has been your experience, then you are more likely to have an emotional and psychological buffer between you and the onslaught of negativity about large bodies that we all encounter as we make our way in the world. This is by no means intended to minimize the damage that size-shaming and the like have done to your self-esteem; it is rather meant to focus attention on the family as a valuable resource—a protective factor[2]—against such damage.

There are also those of us who, for various reasons—among them, family dysfunction, abuse and neglect, significant substance use, and homophobia/transphobia—have not had the protection of our families to shield us from the brutality of size bigotry. If this has been your experience, I would like to invite you to consider what it would be like for you to create "chosen family" for yourself. Chosen families are individuals or groups of people who are a part of our lives with whom we **intentionally** endeavor to create a sense of family. As Currin points out in *Family by Birth and Family by Choice,* their role in our life extends beyond friendship to include full or partial participation in family life, as well as providing mutual support around family responsibilities, such as helping out and providing care.[3] You might already have people in your life who function as chosen family. Whether you do or not, here are some ideas for creating and strengthening these kinds of bonds:

- **Have a formal ceremony as an affirmation of the significance of these relationships in your life.** One option is to seek the services of a life cycle celebrant. They are trained and well-versed in helping people to create meaningful rituals that mark and celebrate the significant events in their lives (for more information on life cycle celebrations, visit http://www.celebrantinstitute.org/). You may also use other clergy members to officiate; have an informal gathering of friends and acquaintances; or have a private ceremony (or ritual) with just you and your chosen family member(s).
- **Create traditions with members of your chosen family.** Traditions serve many meaningful purposes among family members. McKay and McKay noted the role of the family in providing a context for identity development; solidifying the bond among family members; giving comfort and security; instilling values; and adding "to the rhythm and seasonality of life".[4] Anticipating sharing special moments and creating memories with members of your chosen family can go a long way toward supporting your overall sense of wellness.
- **Display pictures of members of your chosen family in your home and/or office, on social media, and as wallpaper and screen savers on your electronic devices.** This is one way of symbolizing their importance in your life. It is a public affirmation of the bond that you share.

- **Make intentional plans to spend time with members of your chosen family during holidays.** Being alone on holidays that people typically gather with family can intensify feelings of loneliness and sadness that can spiral into feelings of despair. Don't let holidays catch you off guard. Anticipate major holidays well in advance, and make concrete, reliable plans to spend some of the time with members of your chosen family. Avoid the pressure of planning traditional celebrations and go with what feels good to you and your chosen family member(s).
- **Be mindful of the pitfalls of building relationships that are based on connecting around a similar trauma history.** There might be a natural tendency to be drawn to these kinds of relationships; after all, who wouldn't want to feel like they are understood by others who have had similar experiences? One way to discern whether there is the potential for a healthy connection with someone with whom you share a similar trauma history is by asking yourself: when I take an honest look at this relationship—putting aside, for the moment, the ways that we support each other around our traumatic histories—am I mostly satisfied or unsatisfied with the quality of the relationship?
- **Keep in mind that not every member of your chosen family will meet all of your relational needs.** Just like in other types of families, the depth of connection that you have with each chosen family member will vary based on many factors, such as: each of your capacity for intimacy; the amount and timing of other demands in your lives; differences in values and interests; and geographical proximity, to name a few.

Romantic Love

Aaah, love. Most of us desire it. For some of us, it seems to flow easily and naturally throughout the cycles of adult life. For others, it seems elusive. Finding and sustaining romantic love can prove a daunting task for many large people, especially women. Our cultural aesthetic around beauty and desire often excludes large bodies. There are a few exceptions among some subcultures in American society. For example, there is a consciousness about body politics and attempts to be inclusive of large bodies among some members of the feminist and queer communities. And various ethnic groups, e.g., Black and some Latinx cultures, as a whole, have historically embraced and celebrated the voluptuousness of large female bodies. I can remember my dad emphatically (if a bit crudely) pronouncing that "nobody but a dog wan' a bone!" However, in mainstream American culture, thinness remains the standard for beauty—and the more that a woman deviates from this standard (i.e. the larger she is), the less likely she is to be thought of as attractive.

Physical attraction is a big part of how many men first evaluate a woman's desirability as a romantic partner. In mainstream American culture, the more that a man aligns with the cultural aesthetic, the less likely he is to consider dating a large woman. And our culture continues to reinforce this: have you ever seen a large woman as a contestant on the reality show, *The Bachelor*? Or as one of the women chosen for a man searching for love on a talk show (unless he, himself, is a large man)? We are completely left out of the equation. In my experience, even some men who are genuinely attracted to large women shy away from developing significant relationships with us because of what they believe their friends, family members, and even society as a whole might think. I have a theory that there are probably more men than we realize who are naturally attracted to women of all sizes; however, cultural ideals shape attitudes from an early age, and by the time that most boys experience that first hormonal surge, they have already drunk the Kool-Aid.

So where does this leave us? There are some things that we, as large women, can do to position ourselves better for satisfying romantic relationships where possibilities exist:

KNOW YOUR WORTH. Consider these points:
- Some of us have been conditioned to believe that if a man expresses interest in us, it is our one and only shot at love. As a result, we might feel like we need to settle for people or behaviors that we do not want (see Chapter 4 for a discussion about being treated with dignity and respect). ***Don't settle.***
- **Believe that you are worthy of love.** For many of us, this will require a close examination of the negative beliefs that we have internalized about ourselves as a result of society's relentless negativity

about large bodies. Many of these beliefs might be so deeply ingrained in us that we are not aware that they are there. But they are. And they affect how we feel about ourselves *and* the energy that we put out into the world. Would-be romantic partners are reading and responding to that energy. If the read is "I am not worthy of love," then the response will likely be, "OK . . . then I will find someone who is." I have added a journal exercise in Appendix B (#1) of this book to help you with identifying and modifying the negative beliefs that you have about yourself as a large woman.

- **Demand respect from people who want to connect with you romantically.** I will talk more specifically about mindful dating in Chapter 6. For now, I encourage you to think about adopting the mindset that doing all of the work—making all of the phone calls (or sending all of the texts or emails), planning all of the dates, giving generously of yourself and asking for little or nothing in return—is not a healthy situation. Try not to judge yourself if you sometimes fall into this behavior. Treating yourself with compassion, kindness, and love will make it less likely that you will in the future.
- **Don't allow yourself to be marginalized.** If a romantic partner is not willing to be with you in public, introduce you to their family and friends, or otherwise invite you into their world, then they do not value you in the way that you deserve to be valued.

As a footnote to the preceding points:

> **TO THE MEN WHO PREY ON LARGE WOMEN** because you know that many of us are wounded: I am putting you on notice that I am spreading the word to my sisters that they deserve MUCH more than you picking at their wounds and feasting on their flesh for sport! Your days of reckless pillaging are numbered.

- **Do your part to challenge and change negative perceptions about large people.** There are lots of ways to do this. Here are some examples:
  - Don't participate in conversations that involve people making disparaging remarks or jokes about large people (even if they are other large people).

- If you feel emboldened enough, challenge and provide corrective information for misperceptions and generalizations about large people (it is perfectly OK if you don't; there is often not enough social support available for people to feel safe enough to do this).
- Support or participate in activities and organizations that promote the fair and equitable treatment of people who live in large bodies.

Self-Love

All too often, the activities that we might be participating in that inspire feelings of love for ourselves are the ones that get the least amount of attention from us. And, in our culture, we are taught that thinking about our own needs is self-indulgent . . . selfish. The reality is that taking care of ourselves better equips us to care for our loved ones, our communities, and the planet. For many of us who have been inundated with negative messages about our size, practicing self-love and self-care does not come naturally, and must be intentionally brought into our awareness for it to manifest. So, I invite you to start a lifelong love affair with yourself, and to treat yourself as well as you would a lover that you want to stick around. Here are some suggestions to get you started:

Take care of your body. Make and keep all of your wellness appointments. Don't put off addressing any health concerns that develop or persist. Ask your healthcare provider which preventive health screenings are recommended for you across your lifespan. Record them and make plans to have them done when indicated.

Embark on a journey of discovery of all the things that contribute to your sense of well-being.
- How do you like to start your day?
- How do you like to wind down at the end of the day?
- Consider whether a pet might bring joy, love, playfulness, and companionship to your life.
- Develop playlists of music that help you to connect with your emotional experience. My latest favorite "love" song for healing old emotional wounds is Sade's *In Another Time* (2010).[5]

- Plan mini breaks throughout a hectic workday (don't forget that caring for children is hard work).
- Breeeeathe.

FOOTNOTES

1. This is a core principle of Object Relations Theory, a theory that was derived from Freudian psychoanalytic theory, as articulated by Scharff, David. E. and Scharff, Jill S., *Scharff Notes: A Primer of Object Relations*. Lanham, MD: Jason Aronson, Inc., 1992.

2. A protective factor is a ". . . condition . . . or attribute . . . in individuals, families, communities[,] or the larger society that help people deal more effectively with stressful events . . . ." (Wikipedia, 2019).

3. Currin, Liz. "Family by Birth and Family by Choice." Atlanta Area Psychological Associates, P. C. 2015, https://www.atlantapsych.com/article/family-birth-and-family-choice.

4. McKay, B. and McKay, K.,"Creating a Positive Family Culture: The Importance of Establishing Family Traditions," The Art of Manliness, http://www.artofmanliness.com/2013/10/09/creating-a-positive-family-culture-the-importance-of-e stablishing-family-traditions/.

5. "In Another Time," CD, track 8 on Sade, *Soldier of Love*, Epic Records, 2010.

CHAPTER FOUR

I HAVE THE RIGHT TO BE TREATED WITH DIGNITY AND RESPECT, REGARDLESS OF MY SIZE.

Empowerment song: *Right Through You*, Alanis Morrisette[1]

In the course of our everyday lives, there are many ways that large women are treated disrespectfully. It happens in ways that are sometimes subtle and unintentional (microaggressions), and then there are times when the dignity of large women is blatantly disregarded. There are also times when we—especially those of us who are in the range of super-sized—might feel disrespected when, in fact, another person is trying to be respectful. When someone looks away to avoid appearing as if they are staring, for example, the action may be well-intentioned, but what they might be communicating to the large person is that they are turning away because they are having a negative reaction to the sight of a super-sized person.

A Closer Look at Microaggressions

Microaggressions occur when someone (or some entity, like a media outlet) says or does something that subtly or unintentionally perpetuates a negative belief or stereotype about members of a marginalized group.[2] While the "micro" part refers to the size of the aggressive act relative to other forms of aggression (e.g., physical violence), my personal experience with being on the receiving end of a microaggression is that they can be incredibly hurtful. It can also be frustrating (to put it mildly) to address or confront them because the other person (or entity) often does not understand the insult in the action—even after it is explained! Here are some examples of microaggressions against large women:

- A friend, after attending a fun party and sharing with you that they had a good time, says to you, ***"Oh, I didn't invite you because I didn't think that you would be interested in going."*** This can be considered a microaggression if the reason that the friend assumed that you were not interested in the party is because they believe that large people are not interested in having social lives.
- ***"Wow*** [with disbelief]***, she is a great athlete!"*** The underlying assumption is that a large person is not capable of being good at sports.
- A person who is thinner than you complaining about their weight in your presence.
- From a romantic prospect, unprompted: ***"I'm OK with the fact that you are a 'big girl.'"***
- _____

Whether or not you confront a microaggression, it is important to your sense of wellness that at least internally, you identify it and acknowledge how it affects you. This will help you to **externalize** the insult, which will help to prevent you from **internalizing** a negative belief about yourself as a result of the microaggression.

Invisibility

Perhaps one of the most common and painful ways that large women are disrespected is in how we are made to feel invisible. It is as if we are the receptacles of society's shame about **everything** that is thought of as flawed and undesirable. We are asked to carry this shame and expected to stay in the shadows of life, lest we remind everyone of something that we are all desperately trying to escape—the reality that, by our very nature as human beings, we are all imperfect. Please don't misinterpret my meaning here: *I* am not saying that being large is a flaw or imperfection, but I am saying that our society has deemed it as such, and because it has, large folks are vulnerable to attack. Because, as a society, we have a very low tolerance for imperfection.

The erasure of large women is evident in the fact that our needs and experiences are woefully absent from public discourse. We are treated as if we will not acquire human status unless and until we lose enough weight to fit the mold that society has created for women. Until then, we are expected to meet our needs with what is available—or do without. Think of a relatively simple problem that many large women deal with—though, if you've ever had it, you know that it is quite unpleasant—skin chafing. Many of us experience chafing in areas of our bodies where friction is created by skin rubbing against skin, often between the thighs. In some circles, folks refer to this as "chub rub" (a term that I absolutely despise, because I believe that it has a *hint* of derision in it, although that is just my opinion). In the past decade or so, a few companies have developed products to prevent and treat this chafing; however, these products are sold in ways that communicate that they are specialty items (e.g., available by online purchase only) rather than just another health and beauty product that is available for women. So, a large woman is unlikely to happen upon one of these products at the drug store; she will likely have to do her own research (as I have) to find them. There is no mainstream advertising of these products, and many of them are marketed as a treatment for skin friction caused by exercising . . . and we *know* that large women don't *exerciiiise* (wink!). If I had to guess, I would say that advertisers probably think of talking about skin chafing in the context of large bodies as something that is shameful and that should remain private—much like how some products that are clearly intended to be used as vibrators are marketed as personal massagers. There is nothing shameful about our large bodies. And we are allowed to live in them with dignity. We deserve to have our needs addressed and our experiences validated through visibility.

Another way that we are treated as if we are invisible is when we are overlooked or excluded from social activities: friendship groups, dating, athletics, competitions, including pageants (not that I am a fan of pageants!). Imagine the toll that all of this takes on our sense of wellness; the damage that this does to our self-esteem is tremendous. And many of us take the banner of neglect and carry it forward. We feel badly about ourselves and our bodies, and we sometimes treat ourselves poorly as a result; we lead a shadowy existence, limiting our participation in certain activities (see Chapter 6 for tips on coming out of the shadows and living a fuller, more satisfying life); we isolate ourselves from relationships with friends, family members, and others; we neglect our own needs. We might even come to believe that we are not worthy of dignity and respect. On the flip side, when we dare to be unapologetic about our bodies and who we are, we are often opening ourselves up to ridicule and bullying.

Once, I was using a shared ride car service, and the other passenger was a young man who was super-sized. Everything about him screamed of shame—as if it was oozing out of his pores. And he seemed to be trying to make himself as invisible as possible: he made no eye contact, he did not greet me when he got into the car, he kept his eyes laser focused on his cell phone for the entire thirty-minute ride, and he seemed preoccupied with making sure that the hem of his coat did not drift over into my seat. I imagined that this was his way of trying not to appear as if he was taking up "too much" space—I've done this myself. I wanted so desperately to say something that would communicate to him, "I see you . . . I respect you . . . you matter to me." I ruled out everything that came to mind because I was worried about sounding patronizing. But I was determined that, before he got out of that car, I was going to say *something*—something to make sure that *this* encounter with humanity did not leave him feeling insignificant. All I could muster was "have a good night!" I feel like this was a missed opportunity to potentially help to shift a large person's experience in the world, if only a tiny bit. In hindsight, even engaging him in small talk about the weather, or the latest Philly happening, would have been preferable to sitting in silence. Perhaps I could have reassured him with a smile and a "you're fine" when he fidgeted with his coat hem. Who knows the breadth of the positive impact this might have had? It might have been the only experience he had that day that reminded him that he is worthwhile. The next time that I find myself in a situation like this, I will be more prepared. I think, however, that at this still early stage in the evolution of our societal attitudes about large bodies, making a direct statement of solidarity around size might make the other person, and me, feel too vulnerable.

> ### Size It Up for Yourself – Journal Entry
>
> - Are there times in your life when, as a result of your size, you have felt invisible around others? If your answer is "yes," what can you do to (respectfully) assert your presence and affirm your dignity and value?
> - What size-related needs of yours have gone unmet because of lack of awareness (or interest) from others—society, family, friends, organizations, and institutions?
> - Are there times when you have been overlooked for, or excluded from, social activities that you believe was because of your size? If your answer is "yes," journal about how you felt about it then, and how you feel about it now. What do you need to emotionally heal from those experiences?
> - Can you think of times when you have been on the receiving end of a microaggression? If your answer is "yes," what do you remember about how it made you feel? Is it important for you to confront the person (or entity) that committed the microaggression? If so, how might you confront them? If not, what do you need to take care of yourself around it?

Media's Treatment of Size

Even in the twenty-first century—where we pride ourselves on being awake and alert to the injustices in society—size bigotry continues to run rampant in movies and on television. Most of the time, large characters are one-dimensional, portrayed as aimless or buffoonish individuals—with an exaggerated focus on food and eating—who exist on the periphery of the lives of the main characters and are hopelessly inept at managing their own lives. These characters' dignity is sacrificed either

(a) to make the protagonist look good; (b) for comic relief when things get too serious; or (c) just for laughs. Even the sitcom *Mike & Molly*[3]—which, by all accounts, was created to provide television viewers with a more positive, realistic narrative about the lives of a large couple who met at an Overeaters Anonymous (OA) meeting (insert eye roll)—routinely includes size-related insults that are leveled at the character Mike and his hapless OA compatriot, Harry. I would not be at all surprised if Melissa McCarthy (who plays Molly) had it written into her contract that she would neither be the target nor the perpetrator of these hurtful barbs.

I have heard some criticism of the storyline for the large character, Kate Pearson, on the television show *This Is Us*[4]—typically that it focuses almost exclusively on her weight.[5] But, from a purely emotional place, actor Chrissy Metz nails what it feels like to be a large woman in America for me. The scene in Season Two, Episode One, when Kate is auditioning to be a singer, tugging on her clothes as she anxiously glances around at the other (cis-sized) women,[6] used to be a scene from my everyday life! Whether we realize it or not, these narratives have a profound impact on how we see ourselves—individually and as a group—and on the extent to which we believe that we deserve to be treated with dignity and respect. In 2018, Internet Movie Database (IMDb) published a list of thirty movies—made from 1979 to 2018—that had either a large person as the main character (as in one of my favorite movies, *Fatso* [1980]) or had themes or sub-themes involving people who live in large bodies.[7] We still have a ways to go for television and movies to feature more accurate, diverse, and dignified portrayals of large people as a matter of course. In the meantime, we can develop a practice of taking these images and stories in with a **critical** eye—deciding for ourselves if what we see reflects what is true for our lives and what we want to believe about ourselves.

Men who Disrespect Large Women

Some cis-sized men enjoy the fantasy, or even the reality, of being with a large woman romantically or sexually, but do not have the desire—or, in some cases, the courage—to be with her publicly. Many of these men treat large women as objects to exploit or fetishize to indulge forbidden passions, or to satisfy inane curiosity. These men are usually all too happy to express desire or love for large women in the shadows—on chat lines, in chat rooms, in sex-only "friendships"—reveling in the things that they love about large women while avoiding the social consequences of having full-fledged, publicly-declared, emotionally-responsible relationships with us.

Many of us, at some point or another, have accepted what singer-songwriter Macy Gray referred to as "crumbs of lovin'"[8] from these types of men. It's OK. If we think about this from a survival perspective, it makes a lot of sense. The human organism is built for survival, and it will do whatever is necessary to meet its basic needs. Our need for love and affection comes as a close third only to our physiological needs (food, water, air, and sleep) and our need for safety and security (e.g., a stable income, adequate housing).[9] If we do not believe that we have access to opportunities for love and affection, we will attempt to get those needs met *by any means necessary*. So, with the underlying (often unconscious) belief that "beggars can't be choosers," we accept what is being offered.

Of course, there are some mitigating factors here. Some large women have always believed that they have the same access to potential romantic partners as anyone else (not this one!). Many have other relationships (e.g., with family members, friends, co-workers) that meet much of their need for love and affection and, therefore, they are less vulnerable to situations that are opportunistic in nature.

One other caveat here: I support and affirm everyone's right to participate in whatever consensual romantic and sexual activities they desire. However, if you are participating in any type of relationship because you do not believe that you have access to something better, or do not believe that you deserve something better, then you might want to consider doing the work of changing or modifying your beliefs. The "Size It Up for Yourself" exercises throughout this book can be a great help.

The Fake Flirt

Another way that the experience of large women is invalidated is by the Fake Flirt (FF). The Fake Flirt is when another person playfully pretends to flirt with a large person. Throughout the FF, it is understood by both parties that there is no real romantic or sexual interest on the part of the person who initiates the flirt. There is an unspoken agreement—an implicit understanding—that it is all in fun. I have seen examples of this on television, in social situations, and I, myself, have been on the receiving end of the FF. In my opinion, the only reason that this is a "thing" is because of the prevailing belief that large people are not thought of as objects of desire; therefore, it is "safe" to pretend to flirt with us because no one (including the person who is flirting) will take it seriously.

How insulting, dehumanizing, and potentially humiliating such a "thing" is! Essentially, if we go along with it (and, in every case that I have ever witnessed, we have), this dynamic forces us to take on the belief that they are on the sidelines of life, part of the background—not even worthy of being taken seriously as a person, let alone as a romantic interest. What might appear to be harmless fun often, in fact, creates feelings of shame and further invisibility and isolation for the recipient.

Size It Up for Yourself – Journal Entry

- Have you ever been on the receiving end of a Fake Flirt? If your answer is "yes," what do you remember feeling while it was happening? What thoughts, feelings, and beliefs are coming up for you now as you reflect on the experience?
- How did you respond to the Fake Flirter's behavior? What do you think, feel, and believe about your response now?
- What, if anything, would you do differently in the situation?

You do not have to "play along" with the Fake Flirt. You have every right to nip it in the bud before it has a chance to pull you in. And there are no rules about how you should do this. My recommendation, however, is that you ask the person to stop directly. This way there is no room for misinterpretation of your wishes or where you stand. If the FF-er (I kind of like that it sounds so close to MF-er) responds by insisting that it is all in good fun, or that you are taking things too seriously, you do not owe them any sort of explanation, argument, or apology. You can simply restate your command (not your wish or desire) for them to **STOP.**

For us, as large women, to be respected by men and women who seek to connect with us romantically and sexually, the old adage holds true:

we must **command** respect. Which, for me, means that we must establish and maintain a "zero tolerance" policy around allowing ourselves to be disrespected. This is not always as easy as it sounds. Please remember that there are times when we, as humans, have competing needs. And sometimes the need for attention, affection—even physical touch—will override the need to be treated with dignity and respect. As yucky as this may sound . . . we are human. And the solution to sometimes choosing these things is to **lovingly** dust ourselves off and get right back to the business of commanding respect. Before you know it, one day you will look up, and you will be saying to yourself, as I did when I was pursued by some cringe-worthy guy online, "thanks, 'dixxthick,' but I am embracing the idea that I deserve more dignity and respect than you have to offer." The following is my adaptation of what the business website *Inc.com* has identified as "4 Simple Habits of People Who Command Respect":[10]

#1: Conduct yourself in a manner that commands respect.
I agree with this recommendation in spirit, but I must add some important modifiers: (a) the notion of "respectability" is very subjective, and it has often been used to try to control the behavior of others who might have a different set of realities and values than society has prescribed; and (b) I believe that **everyone** is deserving of respect. So, careful with this one. If you engage in behaviors that suit you and your lifestyle that are not causing harm to anyone, let your own moral compass be your guide.

#2: Cut out the qualifiers.
People with large bodies might be especially prone to use qualifiers like, "I could be wrong, but" before expressing their thoughts and feelings. Boogaard correctly recognizes this behavior as an attempt to protect the ego (sense of self); our sense of self is constantly under attack, so it makes sense that we might not want to put ourselves completely out there. However, as Boogaard suggests, qualifiers tend to convey a lack of confidence, and we are less likely to be taken seriously when we use them. What qualifiers do you find yourself using?

#3: Learn to accept compliments.
Our culture places a great deal of value on being humble. Many of us are taught not to openly acknowledge the positive things about ourselves from an early age. However, the virtue of humility has a much broader meaning and application in historical contexts[11] than the simple (and

harmless) act of accepting a compliment. Think of it as a way of celebrating yourself and being celebrated by others. If you have a hard time accepting compliments, try experimenting with simply saying "thank you," with a smile, the next time that you are offered one.

#4: Consider what your body language is communicating to others. Regardless of what the words are that are coming out of your mouth, your body language is the ultimate "tell" about what you are thinking and feeling. If your shoulders are hunched over and you have a scowl on your face, how likely is someone to believe it when you say, "It is SO great to meet you!"? Think about what you want to be communicating when you are in the presence of others and adjust your body accordingly.

FOOTNOTES

1. "Right Through You," CD, track 5 on Alanis Morrisette, Jagged Little Pill, Maverick, 1995.

2. Jana, Tiffany and Baran, Michael. Subtle Acts of Exclusion: How to Understand, Identify, and Stop Microaggressions. Oakland, CA: Berrett-Koehler Publishers, Inc., 2020.

3. Roberts, Mark, creator. Mike & Molly. Burbank, CA: Bonanza Productions, 2010.

4. Fogelman, Dan, creator. This Is Us. Los Angeles: Rhode Island Ave. Productions, 2016.

5. Daley, Katerina. "20 Things Wrong with This Is Us We All Choose to Ignore." Screen Rant, January 6, 2019, https://screenrant.com/this-is-us-things-wrong-fans-ignore/.

Miller, Liz Shannon. "7 Fun Body-Positive TV Shows You Can Watch Now (Instead of Netflix's 'Insatiable')." IndieWire, August 12, 2018, https://www.indiewire.com/2018/08/best-body-positive-tv-shows-1201993431/.

Tobin, Taylor. 2019. "Sorry, but 'This Is Us' is Totally Overrated – Here's Why You Can Skip It." Insider, https://www.insider.com/this-is-us-overrated-2018-2.

6. This Is Us, season 2, episode 1, "A Father's Advice," written by Dan Fogelman, featuring Chrissy Metz, aired September 26, 2017, on NBC.

7. anuragsai. "Top 25+ Movies on Over-weight and Obese People." IMDb, last updated September 25, 2019, https://www.imdb.com/list/ls022171306/.

8. "Still," Macy Gray, On How Life Is, Epic Records, 1999.

9. Maslow, Abraham H., "A Theory of Human Motivation," Psychological Review 50, no. 4 (1943): 370 – 96 http://dx.doi.org/10.1037/h0054346.

10. Boogaard, Kat, "4 simple habits of people who command respect," Grow, Inc. April 26, 2016, https://www.inc.com/kat-boogaard/4-simple-habits-of-people-who-command-respect.html.

11. "The Virtue of Humility," Cleverism, updated September 23, 2019, https://www.cleverism.com/virtue-of-humility-leadership/.

CHAPTER FIVE

◆

I HAVE THE RIGHT TO NOT MAKE SELF-DEPRECATING COMMENTS OR JOKES, AND TO LIVE FREE FROM SIZE-RELATED EMBARRASSMENT, HUMILIATON, AND SHAME.

◆

CONTENT WARNING (see the section on content warnings in the preface of this book before reading this chapter.)

What I love about this amendment is that it is mostly self-determined. What I mean by that is: to achieve optimal benefit from adopting it as a belief and practice is not necessarily dependent on the attitudes and actions of others. In some cases, this will mean that it will require less energy and effort to put into practice. In other cases, it will mean that there is less personal vulnerability involved, which might be a reason to make it the first amendment that you commit yourself to; however, there is no prescribed order for integrating the ideas in this book into your life. As with everything in life, of course, other people's responses to your changing attitudes and behaviors will have an impact on you. Here's the exciting part: you get to decide *how much* they do!

Self-Deprecation: What's So Funny? (Part Deux)

In our culture, making self-deprecating comments and jokes has become associated with being humble. It seems to serve as a social lubricant of sorts—taking the intimidation factor out of meeting new people and safeguarding existing relationships from potentially harmful dynamics, like competition. Many of us do it (or have done it). I want to make some very important distinctions here:

Humiliation **is not the same as** humility.

Having a sense of humor **and** making, or allowing yourself to be made, the butt of "fat jokes" **are two very different things**.

Having a sense of humor should generate feelings of happiness, good will and connection, and a healthy sense of pride in oneself. Serving as the butt of a joke will likely leave you feeling worthless, alienated, embarrassed, and ashamed. If there are things about you that are not a core part of your sense of self (e.g., your cooking skills) that you feel are OK to poke fun at, no harm done. But I want to caution you to carefully consider the possibility that you might be so used to not valuing parts of yourself that you might be unaware of the harm that is being done. Consider, for example, laughing at yourself after you realize that you have mispronounced a word, versus saying to someone, "I am so dumb." The first is a light-hearted acknowledgment of how our human imperfections pop up from time to time. The second is a direct assault on a part of one's core sense of self, one's intellect. Which things are safe to poke fun at and which things are not is subjective. Some of us, for example, have experienced emotional injury around something that makes us especially sensitive to it while, on the other hand, someone else might be completely unaffected by the same thing. My advice: when in doubt, err on the side of caution. You are much too important to risk injury when you can potentially avoid it.

Another common way that our comments about ourselves can be self-deprecating is with "diet talk." Diet talk is those seemingly harmless conversations that many women have with each other about what they are eating or are making the decision not to eat ("I shouldn't have that"). It is as if food, for women, has become this enchanted, forbidden thing that we desire, but dare not allow ourselves to enjoy, lest we commit a mortal sin. Food choices have thus become an arbiter of morality for women. I have often observed that large women tend to add an extra layer to diet talk, including not only a confession of their "bad" behavior, but also a statement (or two . . . or three) about the inevitability of their "screw-ups." These statements contain some of the most hateful, contemptuous language that I have ever heard.

Diet talk not only deprives us of the in-the-moment enjoyment of eating food, but it leaves us feeling like bad people for daring to desire it. That feeling likely does not go away after we leave the table. It more likely becomes what psychologist and researcher Francine Shapiro describes as a link in a chain of negative beliefs that we carry about ourselves[1] as the result of the emotional distress caused by berating ourselves for meeting a need as basic and essential as eating food. These beliefs might sound like: "I am weak." "I have no self-control." "I am a failure." "I am greedy (sometimes said or thought with an injection of humor)." "I am ugly." And, if we strip it down even further, things like: "I am bad." "I am not good enough," all of which have the potential, if not certainty, of permeating every part of our lives.

Size It Up for Yourself – Journal Entry

- Do you engage in diet talk?
- What are some of the things that you say to yourself and others when you do?
- What feelings come up when you say these things?
- What might be the deeper, more damaging, message that you are sending to yourself when you say these things?
- Would you like to make a commitment to yourself to avoid engaging in diet talk whenever you can?

Liberating Yourself from Embarrassment, Humiliation, and Shame

The summer before my freshman year of high school, my mother and all but one of her six siblings, by then scattered up and down the Eastern Seaboard, traveled with their families to my aunt and uncle's home on Long Island for an extended family reunion barbeque. It was a joyous day, filled with love and celebration of family. At some point, my cousin and I were sitting at a table eating, and I noticed that she had a barbequed rib on her plate. I said something like, "Ooh! We have ribs?!"

An adult relative who had been standing nearby came over to me, leaned down, poked me in the side and said, in the most affected, syrupy Southern drawl, "Shuuuugah, don't you have enough ribs already?" Not being one to back down from an attack, I quickly—with much sarcasm—shot back, "I think I need one more to complete the set." However, in an instant, the bubble of safety and love and belonging that I had been floating in all day was gone. And it was replaced by a river of shame and humiliation that I continued to drown in for years. I no longer felt safe and happy; this person stole that from me. And what a time in my life for them to do it: I was *just* starting to experience my body in relation to other people's bodies. I had my first serious interest in a boy that summer.

I am imagining that many of you have similar stories to tell. This, and other experiences of being embarrassed, humiliated, and shamed about my body, had a tremendous impact on how I felt about myself and my place in the world. I started high school believing that there were many experiences that would not be available to me: dating, fashion (and my school was known for being particularly fashionable), cheerleading—or any extra-curricular activities at all, for that matter. And I made that my reality. For my entire freshman year, one of the most popular (and handsome) boys in school—a Senior!—would take every opportunity to show me that he was interested in me. However, that did not fit with my schema—my mental blueprint—for who I was in the world. So, I ignored him. There were even times when I physically ran away from him as he called after me.

> ### Size It Up for Yourself – Journal Entry
>
> - What have been your experiences around being embarrassed, humiliated, and shamed about your size?
> - How have they impacted what you think and how you feel about yourself?
> - How have they affected how you live your life?
> - How can you begin to separate the negative thoughts, feelings, beliefs, and behaviors that you have developed as a result of these experiences from your "original" core sense of self, which likely still holds the memory of all that is good about you?

Try this mindfulness exercise:
Find a comfortable place with no distractions to sit or lie down, where your body feels fully supported and able to relax.

Once you have settled in, take a slow, gentle breath in through your nose and allow it to travel slowly and gently down to your belly. Allow it to linger there for a second or two before slowly and gently releasing it back up and out through your nose. Repeat this a few times—reminding yourself that there is nothing else that you need to be doing right now—until you feel that you are in a deeper state of relaxation. This will allow you to do this exercise with a clearer mind.

Now bring up one of the negative thoughts, feelings, beliefs, or behaviors that have become a part of your life as the result of being embarrassed, humiliated, or shamed about your size.

What would you like to do with it? There are endless options available to you.

- You could use your imagination to toss it into a fire and watch it disintegrate until there is nothing left.
- You could store it in a vessel of your choosing and then decide what you want to do with it. Do you want to take it somewhere and release it into the atmosphere to be recycled into new, more positive energy? Do you want to dispose of it in some way?

The important thing here is that **you are making a distinction between this negative thought, feeling, belief, or behavior and YOU,**

who is unblemished and capable of accessing goodness. Take as much time as you need.

When you are ready, search inside yourself for a more positive thought, feeling, belief, or behavior to replace it with. Breathe this in. Enjoy the feeling of embracing something new and positive. Remind yourself that this new experience is available to you any time that you need it.

When you are ready, slowly begin to become aware of your surroundings. Notice the sensations of the various parts of your body, the places where they are making contact with the chair, or the bed. Notice your feet on the floor or the ground if you are sitting. As you reconnect with the present, continue to allow these new possibilities to be available to you.

FOOTNOTES

1. Shapiro, Francine. *Eye Movement Desensitizaion and Reprocessing (EMDR): Basic Principles, Protocols, and Procedures.* 2nd ed. New York: The Guilford Press, 2001.

CHAPTER SIX

I HAVE THE RIGHT TO FULLY ENGAGE IN ALL OF THE PHYSICAL, EMOTIONAL, AND SOCIAL (INCLUDING ROMANTIC LOVE) ACTIVITIES OF LIFE AT THE SIZE THAT I AM NOW—WITH OR WITHOUT ANY PLANS TO MAKE CHANGES TO MY SIZE OR WEIGHT.

In American culture, there is a common misperception that large people are either incapable of or not interested in participating in many of the activities that give life meaning and add to our sense of happiness and well-being. Sadly, there are even those among us who believe that large people are not deserving of such full participation in life. Nothing could be further from the truth! Body size does not determine our potential for living full and active lives. However, many of us have been duped into believing that it does. For some of us, this belief first develops when, as children, we are excluded because of our size from team sports, extracurricular classes, clubs, or other group activities. In other cases, we take our cues from what we see in the world around us; as I mentioned earlier, most of the images that we are exposed to in the media perpetuate negative stereotypes of large people as being inactive and disconnected from the mainstream of life.

You deserve full and active participation in life—in whatever shape or form you want your life to take, based on your own unique likes, dislikes, desires, needs and, yes, limitations (we all have them!). And—get this: you are deserving of that right now! Those of us who have a history of body dissatisfaction, shame, and/or loathing are particularly vulnerable to getting caught up in what has been called **destination addiction.**

End Destination Addiction (Right) Now!

Destination addiction (a term coined by Dr. Robert Holden, founder of the United Kingdom's Happiness Project) is, as one writer aptly described it, "a preoccupation with the idea that happiness is in the next place, the next job . . . with the next partner [and so on] . . . ."[1] It keeps us focused on the future and robs us of the opportunity to truly connect with the people, places, and things that could be giving us joy in the moment.

The dieting mindset and the diet industry have reinforced this idea: "when I am thinner, I will be happy . . . I will find love . . . I will ride a rollercoaster . . . I will wear a bikini . . . etc., etc., etc." What would it be like if we were to abandon the idea that happiness is somewhere out there on the horizon and instead embrace the moments of our lives with an openness to everything that they have to offer? This might mean that, at times, we will experience difficult emotions like anger (or rage), sadness, grief, disappointment, and loneliness. But the likelihood is that there will be many, many other times when we will be able to appreciate and partake in the sumptuousness of life.

Following are some suggestions for how you can end destination addiction (now!):

- **Be intentional about how you engage with the everyday things that are happening in your life.** I'll admit: when I am trudging through a monotonous task—like washing dishes, for example—I enjoy a good distraction like music, or even a phone chat with a friend. But what about other times? Like taking a warm, soothing, scented bath. Playing with your children. Eating a strawberry. Do you take time to really savor the moments of the experience? Do you offer gratitude? Do you allow yourself to become fully immersed in the experience?
- **Make a list of the things that you have been putting off doing**

until _____. Ask yourself: is it (f)actually true that you have to wait until you have more money, the kids are older, you have more free time, the planets are aligned? Or is this just another stalling technique that keeps you from experiencing the richness of life? Don't put off enjoying your life *ONE SECOND LONGER*. Work to remove the barriers that keep you from doing the things on your list and make plans to do them as soon as possible.

- **Examine your beliefs about how worthy you are to experience the fullness of life.** Some of us are completely aware that we suffer from poor self-esteem and feelings of low self-worth. For others of us, these negative beliefs about ourselves have become so embedded in our nervous systems that we are acting them out in ways that undermine our happiness *without even knowing it*. If you suspect that this might be the case for you, developing a relationship with a good therapist or wellness coach—where you can dedicate time to exploring and modifying your beliefs—is a great option.
- **Consider starting some type of mindfulness practice.** Mindfulness practice involves developing a routine of behaviors and activities that are aimed at focusing your awareness on the present moment. There are lots of options out there to get you started—from listening to mindfulness-based CDs and downloads, to attending yoga classes or meditation groups, to enrolling in a mindfulness workshop or course. Whatever you choose, keep in mind that, just like any practice, it will take time and effort to get good at it. (For more information about mindfulness practice, see the section on mindful dating later in this chapter.)

As I alluded to earlier, the most important thing that you can do to end destination addiction is to decide that you are worth it. Many of us need support in getting there, so don't hesitate to reach out for positive sources of support: nurturing and affirming relationships; community resources like groups and workshops; one-on-one counseling. It is particularly important for people who live in large bodies to connect with affirming messages about size. The Internet, along with the Resources section of this book, are great resources for this.

Let's Get Physical

Even when we, as large folks, are capable of and interested in physical activity, we sometimes shy away from it because we fear judgment and ridicule from others. Ironically, many of the people who will bully large folks about not exercising (an assumption) are the same people who will look at a large person who dares to go to a gym as if to say, "what are YOU doing here?" And, as a culture, we have linked physical activity so much to the goal of losing weight that many of us no longer enjoy movement for the sake of movement. I remember an experience that I had one summer when I was in college: I was working as a recreational counselor at a residential treatment facility for adolescents with behavioral health problems. On this particular day, we had taken the youth on an outing to Brandywine Creek State Park for a day of canoeing. As soon as the trip was announced, I felt my anxiety begin to build. Before I started aerobic walking some ten or so years ago, I had suffered near-constant pain in my knees for as long as I could remember. With the pain came stiffness and a lack of flexibility, which made the idea of balance feel like a virtual impossibility. During those years, I would have been far too embarrassed to ask for the kind of assistance that I needed to get into a canoe. I stood on the dock and watched one duo after another nimbly board their assigned canoes. When my turn came, I told myself to "just get it over with"—as I often have at times when I have been faced with a challenge that I felt that I would not be able to overcome. I stepped into the canoe without much attention to balance—and into the creek I went! The staff and the youth all roared with laughter. After I got the help that I needed, my canoeing partner, a thirteen- or fourteen-year-old girl with oppositional behaviors, spent the rest of the trip trying to intentionally tip our canoe.

As much as I tried to just shake off my embarrassment, humiliation, and shame, the feelings invaded my body, mind, and soul like a cancer. I continued on with the day, re-engaging with my beloved co-workers. I attempted to regain my good-natured authority with the youth. It even registered with me that, in spite of it all, I really love canoeing. But inside, I felt so diminished. In moments like this, almost . . . *almost* . . . everything that I had gained in terms of believing that I had value would temporarily float away, and I would convince myself that the only way that I would truly be acceptable is if I became thin. So, I would join my cis-sized friends in diet and exercise talk, and I would wait, in a swamp of shame, for my life to begin. How might my experience have been different that day if I had felt safe enough to shamelessly ask for the help I needed to board the canoe?

> ### Size It Up for Yourself – Journal Entry
>
> - How would you move your body if you had no fear of embarrassment, humiliation, or shame?
> - If you took a moment and allowed yourself to believe in endless possibilities (even if it does not feel realistic . . . just try it!), what physical activities would spark your interest and excite your imagination? Would they be athletic? Creative (like dance or improvisation, for example)? Would you add new movements or activities to your sexual repertoire? (I am happy to report that quite a few books and articles have been written about sexual positions for large people!)
> - If any of the activities that you listed from the previous question would be difficult to do because of physical challenges and limitations, could you modify it to make some version of it possible? I was excited to learn recently that the premier ice-skating rink in my city has partnered with one of the local rehabilitation centers to offer sled skating for children and adults with physical disabilities—free of charge!
> - What kind of support do you need to make it happen? Do you need a friend to join you (or cheer you on from the sideline)?

The Quest for Romantic Love

For many large women, dating and partnering is one of the biggest life challenges that we face. Many of us must work to overcome negative beliefs that we hold about ourselves (e.g., that we are not attractive or beautiful) only to find that some prospective dating partners hold similar beliefs about us. We often walk the tightrope of trying to summon the confidence to put ourselves out there—confidence that we might feel in spades in other areas of our lives—while wrestling with the persistent torment of not feeling quite good enough. Add to this the fact that there is no shortage of men who are all too willing to take advantage of us because they believe that we are desperate and that we will accept any kind of treatment that they give us. Yikes! I can feel the weight of it all as I am typing this.

Mindful Dating

One way to improve your experience with dating as a large woman is to incorporate some of the basic tenets of mindfulness practice into your approach. Mindfulness involves focusing on what is happening in the present moment—in your body, your mind, and in the world around you.[2] As a concept, this might seem simple. However, most of us spend a great deal of our time with our thoughts focused on the past, both recent and distant, and the future. Take, for example, something as routine as taking a shower. Is your attention usually fully focused on what is happening in the moment? Are you tuned in to the smell of your body wash? The feel of the water as it hits the various parts of your body? The sounds around you: the hum of the exhaust fan, the sound of the water beating against the shower wall, the basin, or the curtain? Or is your awareness of those things in the background, as thoughts of the phone call that you had with your mother last night, or what time you need to leave the house to get to your appointment on time, take center stage?

The basic practice of "tuning in" to what is happening in and around you can serve you well in the world of dating. You might start by bringing your awareness to what is happening in your body **the first time** that you make contact with a potential dating partner—whether this happens online, over the phone, or in person (see Mindful Dating Checklist below). By tuning in to your body, you will discover what your **authentic** first impressions of the person are. Your "gut" will have already begun to signal you about whether it detects that you are entering into friendly territory, or that there are "red flags" present. For various reasons, we sometimes ignore the signals that our body gives us. For example, we might be distracted by a person's physical attractiveness. We might believe that anyone showing interest in us is a fluke, and that we cannot afford to pass up the opportunity. Or we might be weary of searching for a suitable partner and therefore make the conscious decision to settle for what is before us.

Mindful Dating Checklist

First Contact:
☐ in person ☐ over the phone ☐ online

What does your "gut" tell you about this person **after the first five (5) minutes** of conversation?

_____
_____
_____

Where do you feel this in your body? (check as many as apply)
☐ Head ☐ Face ☐ Neck ☐ Shoulders
☐ Arms ☐ Chest ☐ Stomach ☐ Back
☐ Legs ☐ Feet ☐ Other: _____

RED FLAGS (things that give you pause):
_____
_____
_____
_____

TABLE 6.1: Mindful Dating Checklist

Learning to listen to and trust your gut is one of the most valuable life skills that you can acquire. There is a caveat here, though. Sometimes we can confuse our gut—our natural, basic instincts—with other things. For example, we have all developed mental strategies to help us to cope with pain and distress. These are sometimes referred to as adaptations. The fear of isolation and rejection can lead us to activate several maladaptive (unhelpful) coping strategies: we might lower our expectations of potential partners and accept poor treatment. We might be attracted to what has been familiar, especially as it resembles the couple relationships that have been modeled for us early in our lives by our family members, our culture, our community, and the media that we consume. And if we have been treated poorly by romantic partners in the past, we might have come to believe that being treated poorly in relationships is normal, or all that we deserve.

> ### Size It Up for Yourself – Journal Entry
>
> - What are the self-defeating ways that you have changed your behavior and/or expectations (ignored your gut) to allow a romantic partner into your life?
> - What are some "life-giving" practices that you can replace them with?
>
> The more awareness that you have (the more mindful you are) about the things that are influencing your reactions and choices, the more confident you will be in them. The more confident you are about your instincts and choices, the more confidence you will project into the world.

FOOTNOTES

1. Griffiths, Mark D., "The Search for Happiness: A Brief Look at "Destination Addiction" *Psychology Today* (blog), July 20, 2016, https://www.psychologytoday.com/us/blog/in-excess/201607/the-search-happiness.

2. Kabat-Zinn, Jon. *Wherever You Go, There You Are: Mindfulness Meditation in Everyday Life*. New York: Hyperion, 1994.

CHAPTER SEVEN

◆

I HAVE THE RIGHT TO WEAR WHATEVER I CHOOSE, AND TO ADORN MY BODY IN A MANNER THAT FEELS GOOD TO ME, REGARDLESS OF WHAT OTHERS MIGHT THINK.

◆

"The clothes should fit **you**, Auntie . . . not the other way around."
— paraphrased from my niece, Michelle, at age eighteen, while we were out shopping for clothes for my father's funeral

It is only in the past few decades that fashionable clothing and accessories in large sizes have been available to the masses. I can remember a time when, unless we made our own clothes or had them made for us, large women had very limited options if we wanted to be stylish. Anyone over forty will probably remember the stretchy polyester pants with the wide elastic waistband and the sewn-in seam that ran down the front of the pant leg that was a staple in most large women's wardrobes. Even today, I am crushed when I am shopping in a store that primarily stocks cis-sized clothing—usually with a small "WOMENS PLUS" section toward the back—to find that an item that makes my heart skip a beat is not available in my size.

With the advent of the size acceptance movement, and later the Internet, more and more retailers that "specialize" in clothing and accessories for large women have cropped up. However, they are still not as readily accessible as cis-sized clothing retailers. If, for example, I need a blouse for an event that is taking place the next day, I usually do not have multiple options for finding one that I like on the spur of the moment. I cannot count the number of times that I have shuttled back and forth between Lane Bryant and Avenue, trying to find exactly (or, at least, close to) what I was looking for, only to end up settling for what was available. Thank goodness, things are changing. And it appears that many more people are embracing a more positive narrative about what it means to live in a large body, and are celebrating their bodies by taking advantage of the growing number of stylish clothing options that are available.

My own experience around taking advantage of this progress has been complicated by some of the beliefs that I have internalized about myself from society, in general, and from my experiences in my family, in particular. My first memories of being treated differently because of my size are from my elementary school years. I have fragments of a memory of being in Strawbridge & Clothier with my mother and hearing her tell me that I could not get the awesome tartan skirt with the giant safety pin on the side that I wanted *so badly* because an A-line skirt would be more "becoming" on me. To this day, I still don't exactly know what an "A-line" is, but I knew that it was NOT what I wanted! I remember being aware that my cousin, who was larger than me, was allowed to wear what was trending at the time to our school's Dress Up Day, and I had to wear what my mother deemed to be "becoming." Thus began my love-hate relationship with buying clothes.

Fast forward to the present and . . . I rarely shop for clothes for myself. (Post-script: since this writing, I have started to buy a lot more clothing that I love and that fits well.) It is not that I don't like clothes; in fact, it might even be accurate to say that I love them. But, in many ways, I am still haunted by the ghosts of the past. The message that I internalized about myself and my body was that I am not worthy of looking and feeling good in my clothes. This belief was further reinforced when I *did* find clothes that I loved in my size and they were all made to fit a shape that is not like mine. I am five feet, eleven inches tall. Most of my weight is concentrated in my midsection, and I have thin arms and legs and narrow hips. I also have very large breasts and a flat bottom.

When I am forced to shop for clothes, the scene is always the same: I browse the carefully arranged clothing displays (typically, the clothes are wrapped around the hangers to appear smaller and to replicate an hourglass shape) and I feel a cautious excitement as I amass the ten or so items that begin to weigh down my arm. My anxiety begins to build as I ask for a dressing room. Once inside, I arrange the clothes on the available hooks, take a deep breath . . . and a seat. After a minute or so, I stand up and I look at my body in the full-length mirror. I am suddenly aware of how seldom I do this. Over the years, I have gone from feeling absolute horror and disgust at the sight of my body to reminding myself to look through and then past the lenses that were forced upon me—in order to discover my own perceptions of my body. Feeling better now, I start to try on clothes. I have taught myself to slow down at this point, because my inclination is to rush through this part as quickly as possible. So, I tug on pants that either fit perfectly on my legs and do not make it around my belly, or that fasten nicely around my waist and swallow my legs whole.

I tend to have a slightly better experience with shirts and blouses: I can usually find styles that provide fairly good overall coverage, except many are too short (relative to my height) and are less of a custom fit on me than they would be on someone with smaller breasts. When I was a child, Lane Bryant was more like a small department store. My mother, at five foot ten inches and about 140 lbs., used to shop in their "Tall" department. There was also a department that did alterations. By the time that I was wearing large clothing sizes, this and other departments (formal wear, outerwear, swimwear, intimate apparel, bargain basement) had been phased out, and their flagship store in Philadelphia had shrunk from four floors to one. According to the International Directory of Company Histories,[1] these changes were the result of Lane Bryant's acquisition by The Limited Stores, Inc. Along with these changes came a "one size (and shape) fits all" mentality that seems to prevail . . . mostly. I have seen some attempts, in recent years, to offer some very basic styles (e.g., jeans and trousers) in a variety of cuts, with names like classic, relaxed, slim, athletic. Progress.

This discussion of clothing and fashion might seem somewhat trivial when compared to some of the other topics in this book, like wellness and basic human rights. My belief, however, is that how we feel in the clothes that we wear directly affects how we feel about ourselves, and the energy that we put out into the world. When we feel good about what we are wearing, we are more likely to feel good in our skin, and to move our bodies in ways that reflect that: upright posture, shoulders back, a lightness in our gait . . . we exude confidence and well-being. From this confident vantage point, our lens automatically adjusts to take in the goodness that is all around us. Possibilities emerge. And others are drawn to this positive energy.

On the other hand, when I do not feel good about what I am wearing, I feel a bit like a snail having just been doused with salt: I shrivel and I shrink. Before I know it, I have already entered *the rabbit hole*, and the spiral of negative self-perceptions begins. Suddenly, it is not just that my shirt does not fit well. I am also unattractive, I am not good at my work, people don't enjoy my company, and so on, and so on. Your experience may be more or less extreme, but you are likely to have your own brand of negative thinking bubbling just beneath the surface. While we are on the subject of fit, I would be remiss if I did not disclose that it has only been in the past year or so that I have put the energy into finding bras that truly fit me. In the past, I have not valued myself and my body enough to wade through the quagmire of seemingly endless Internet searches, or to trek down to the only custom bra shop that carries large sizes that I am aware of, despite living in the fifth largest city in America! I had been experiencing a collision of my own limiting beliefs about myself, and the inaccessibility of garments that fit me properly. I had also been carrying the inaccurate belief that I needed to wear clothes that hide my large belly. I am now adamant that my large belly is as much a part of who I am as any other part of me. And if my young niece—who loved and snuggled my belly with such enthusiasm—can find beauty and enjoyment in it, then why can't I?

The moral of this story is that you deserve to wrap the gift of the one precious body that you have been given in whatever packaging you choose. Some of us have found safe spaces, e.g., BBW events, where we allow ourselves to strut unabashedly, wearing the things that we love and that make us happy. Is it time for you to take it to the next level? No one can answer this question but you. Only you know the impact that opening yourself up to potential scrutiny will have. My latest self-care activity is to have my clothes altered to fit my body the way that I want them to. What changes do you want to make to improve your relationship with what you wear?

Cis-sized Entitlement

There seems to be an attitude among a segment of our society that only cis-sized people should be allowed to wear certain things. Like bikinis. Or any other body-revealing clothing, for that matter. This attitude is a form of **entitlement**, not unlike other forms of entitlement. Some cis-sized people believe that it is OK to give looks of disapproval or disdain when they see a large person wearing something that they do not think that they "should" be wearing. Some are even so bold as to audibly verbalize their opinion. They seem to believe that large people are not entitled to the same dignity and respect (see Chapter 4) as everyone else. And a large woman might be reluctant to call someone out on their bad behavior because (as discussed in Chapter 2) she might fear that no one will come to her defense. Or even worse, that the situation might escalate. She might wonder: will others join in? Will the agitator become violent? Or she might be so accustomed to this kind of treatment that she believes, on some level, that she deserves it.

Many of us—whether we live in large or cis-sized bodies—wish to wear things that we believe are flattering—to our body, for the shape of our face, for our complexion, for our age, etc. And there is nothing wrong with that.[2] The problem comes in when any of us believes that we have the right to decide for someone else what is appropriate for them to wear. This right belongs exclusively to the wearer. My or your opinion is completely irrelevant to another person's decision to wear what feels good to them.

> ### Size It Up for Yourself – Journal Entry
>
> Think about how you feel when you like (or love) what you are wearing **versus** times when you do not feel good about what you are wearing. You might want to create a chart in your journal to record your thoughts and feelings. In each case,
> - How do you feel about yourself?
> - How do you carry your body?
> - How do you engage with others?
> - What do you believe about yourself?

More on Size Exclusion in Retail

Recently, I was online searching for a winter coat to wear over my sweaty post-exercise clothes. A Google search quickly turned up the perfect coat from Lululemon, a *chichi* Canadian athletic apparel retailer that actually has a store in my city. While I was fairly certain that they do not carry large sizes, I decided to check anyway. I discovered through a second Google search that not only does the store top out at size fourteen, but that, according to consumer advocates and former employees, it is an intentional part of their marketing strategy to only promote sizes eight and below.[3]

As shocking as this may seem, it is not a new phenomenon in the fashion industry. For decades, there have been designers who absolutely *refuse* to design clothes for large women; some say that we will not look the way that they want us to look in their clothes, while one designer blatantly said, "No one wants to see curvy women" modeling designer clothes.[4] Listen closely to what they are saying. They would rather lose money—according to Forbes magazine, upwards of $46 billion a year as of 2016[5]—than to see their designs on large women. That is the height of size phobia.

If some designers were to claim that they are asserting their right to freedom of artistic expression by not designing clothes for large bodies (even though any thoughtful person knows that this is about perpetuating America's propaganda, if you will, about size), then they should be designing clothes for museum exhibitions—and not for consumers! Of course, we cannot (for the most part) legislate what people produce and sell. However, we can find ways to have a significant *enough* impact on sales that they rethink their exclusionary practices. Here are some suggestions on how:

- If clothing designers and retail outlets do not care about our dollars, we can enlist the support of our cis-sized allies in boycotting companies that do not make clothes in large sizes.
- We, ourselves, can make a commitment to not patronize businesses that exclude large clothing sizes. For example, I have a cis-sized classmate in my body weight training/yoga class who gives me a ride to the train station every week. I wanted to give her a token of my appreciation and, since I know that she likes stylish exercise clothes, I thought about getting her a gift certificate to—guess where—Lululemon. After finding out about their discriminatory practices, there is no way that they will get *one thin dime* from me. We can choose to not buy for others, or purchase items that do not depend on size (not one sock, not one glove) from these companies.

Do you have your own unique way that you would like to protest this injustice?

During the time that I was writing this book, I had a rare evening when I finished work early enough to go shopping for a handbag. As someone who hardly ever shops for myself, I was bubbling over with excitement as I made my way to the nearby shopping district. After not finding anything that I liked at a department store outlet, I happened upon a moderately sized women's clothing boutique. For my entire adult life, I have avoided these kinds of stores. Most do not sell clothes and shoes that are outside of the range of cis sizes. But I knew from the window display that this store would probably have a handbag that I liked. I felt my hesitation as I crossed the street and approached the door. Once inside, I felt like I was a foreigner in a strange land. I imagined that people were stealthily looking at me, wondering why I had come into *this* store. As I tried to appear natural and unaffected, I began to peruse the merchandise. My eyes fell wistfully on a beautiful suede patchwork mini skirt. I fought off a familiar thought: "I'll be able to shop in stores like this when I lose weight." The thought came automatically, unsummoned, despite the fact that I have managed to archive these kind of thoughts in recent years. Reflecting on it now, I am aware that it was the environment itself that set me up to re-enter the space of self-loathing and feelings of inferiority. No handbag—or anything else—is worth the annihilation of self that occurs *just by entering these spaces*. I invite you to consider whether it is worth it to you.

FOOTNOTES

1. Grant, Tina. International Directory of Company Histories. Vol. 64. St. James Press, 2004.

2. Although there is probably some implicit bias lurking in our assessments of what is flattering for us to wear, e.g., when we choose things that are meant to hide parts of ourselves that we think of as "flaws."

3. Bhasin, Kim, "Shunning Plus-Size Shoppers is Key to Lululemon's Strategy, Insiders Say," Huffpost, July 31, 2013, https://www.huffpost.com/entry/lululemon-plus-size_n_3675605.

4. Gunn, Tim, "Tim Gunn: Designers Refuse to Make Clothes to Fit American Women. It's a Disgrace," The Washington Post, September 8, 2016, https://www.washingtonpost.com/posteverything/wp/2016/09/08/tim-gunn-designers-refuse-to-make-clothes-to-fit-american-women-its-a-disgrace/.

5. Weinswig, Deborah. "Will J.Crew Announcement Disrupt the $46 Billion Women's Plus-Size Market?" Retail. Forbes. July 20, 2018. https://www.forbes.com/sites/deborahweinswig/2018/07/20/a-land-grab-is-likely-under-way-for-the-46-billion-womens-plus-size-market-opportunity/?sh=6b-38c7d43489.

CHAPTER EIGHT

*I HAVE THE RIGHT TO
REASONABLE ACCOMMODATIONS IN
PUBLIC SPACES, SUCH AS SEATING THAT IS
COMFORTABLE AND SUPPORTIVE.*

I remember visiting the Betsy Ross House, near where I live in Philadelphia, sometime after I had reached the height that I am now. It was interesting to notice that, throughout the house, at almost six feet tall, I had to bend over to avoid hitting my head on the ceiling. I hypothesized that in the 1700s, adults must have been much shorter than they are today. After surveying the research on Colonial architecture, my theory did not hold up. The bandbox style of homes—like the one where Betsy Ross lived when she famously worked as a flag maker—was constructed on the smaller side to make it affordable for the growing population of working-class Philadelphians.[1] My erroneous assumption aside, it got me to thinking: the objects that we use to support and enhance our living should be designed to accommodate our needs, and not the other way around.

As a large person, I have often felt ashamed and embarrassed when I did not fit comfortably into seating—at restaurants, on airplanes, in classrooms, in theaters. I have watched as others have seemed to feel embarrassed and uncomfortable on my behalf. This kind of empathy is unquestionably well-intentioned; however, it implicitly gives legitimacy to the idea that there is something to feel embarrassed and uncomfortable *about*. The notion that everyone should be able to fit into a single-sized world is absurd. It is not only towering NBA stars who should have their size-related needs—like custom-built countertops to accommodate their height—met. We, as large people, deserve to have our needs reasonably accommodated as well.

The difference between these two groups is that, as a society, we do not make the same value judgments about height. We *do* judge. For example, short men are sometimes judged to be less masculine, or are not taken seriously. However, the same barriers to fitting comfortably into everyday spaces that plague many large people are unlikely to exist. Adjustments that are made to accommodate the ways that different people take up space (e.g., for a person in a wheelchair) are not perceived to be the result of the person's moral failing. Think about this: at most airlines, a large person who does not fit safely in an airplane seat will be required to purchase an extra seat to accommodate their size.[2] Tall people have the option of requesting seats with extra leg room. Imagine if a person with a different kind of physical limitation were forced to pay extra to accommodate their space-related needs. The Americans with Disabilities Act (ADA) folks would be all over it! As well they should be.

Thanks to the efforts of size advocacy groups like NAAFA, airlines are now required to provide seat belt extenders for passengers who need them. (**Note:** In 2012, the Federal Aviation Administration [FAA] banned the use of seat belt extenders that are purchased independently by passengers, citing the fact that they have not been inspected by the FAA and, therefore, may not meet safety requirements.[3]) So, if we as a group are loud enough, we can facilitate change. In recent years, I have also been in an increasing number of waiting rooms at hospitals and doctor's offices that have at least one wider chair available for large patients' comfort.

At this point, I want to digress for a moment to address a serious issue. As a frequent user of rideshare car services, I have often seen large folks riding or driving without a seat belt on. Now, as a large person, I understand what it is like to struggle to secure my body (and not strangle myself in the process!) in a seat belt. And there was a time when I would have skipped wearing one altogether to avoid feeling embarrassed and ashamed. I am also aware that for some of you, a seat belt will not fit at all. But here's the thing: **Your safety matters. You matter.** Nationwide, the use of seat belts saves an estimated 14,955 lives per year.[4] Your life is *way* more important than whatever feelings you experience as the result of struggling to fasten your seat belt or whipping out a seat belt extender to make your ride safe and comfortable. I am at the point now where I will wriggle and squirm for as long as it takes to get the belt around me and securely fastened—even *if* an obnoxious twenty-something is probably texting about me to her friend from the other passenger seat. An interesting thing happened after I started believing that I deserved to be as safe as I could be, no matter what it took: the embarrassment and shame went away. Not only did those feelings go away, but I now feel a rush of pride every time I put on a seat belt—knowing that it is a simple act that symbolizes my belief in my own worth.

In response to two separate petitions made by individuals who could not use the seat belts in their vehicles, in 2003, the National Highway Traffic Safety Administration published a list of car makers who either have longer seat belts standard in their vehicles, or who make optional seat belt extenders available.[5] This is progress; however, it only addresses the needs of folks who can afford to buy a new car. Thinking about it now, it is disgraceful—criminal, even—that car makers are not required to equip cars with seat belts that are long enough to fit *all* bodies. This is yet another way that the needs and experiences of large people are overlooked and undervalued in our society. What I have learned during my years on the planet is that, unfortunately, most changes in the direction of fairness and justice don't happen simply because they are fair and just; they happen because those who are being treated unfairly and unjustly, along with their allies, start to demand change. Before we can begin to demand grand scale, sweeping change, we must believe that we deserve it. When I, at age fourteen, had my very first job—at a recreation center for people with physical and intellectual disabilities—the city's mass transit system had just started to implement the policies that were fought for and won by people with disabilities through Section 504 of the 1973 Rehabilitation Act.[6] As is often the case with changes that occur in a top-down fashion, it was some time before all of the bus drivers started to adhere to the law, and some of our campers who used wheelchairs were often left at the side of the road as a bus that was equipped with a wheelchair lift drove by. These folks did not rest on their laurels; they made phone calls. And wrote letters. Until . . . things . . . changed. And that is likely what it will take for large people to gain "equal access" in *all* public spaces.

> ### Size It Up for Yourself – Journal Entry
>
> - What have been some of your embarrassing, humiliating—or just physically uncomfortable—experiences around seating?
> - What about access: for example, a step that was too high to clear or step down from, or narrow walkways and doorways?
>
> Here are some things that you can do to improve your experience (in the process, you might even be furthering the cause of equal access for all!):
>
> - One of the first things that you can do when you are confronted with a situation in which your size-related needs are not being adequately met is to mentally step out of the situation for a moment and take an inventory of your feelings. If you notice that you are feeling embarrassed or ashamed, ask yourself why. "What am I doing wrong?" I can answer that question for you: absolutely nothing. There is nothing morally (or otherwise) wrong with being a large person. As Chapter 12 will expand on, we all have the right to respectfully take up space.
> - Find out if there are ways to have your size-related needs accommodated. For example, is there another seating option available (a table instead of a booth, for example)? Is there an entrance that has a ramp? Practice asking for what you need with confidence—even if you have to fake it in the beginning.
> - Whenever possible, don't patronize businesses that do not provide at least one option for comfortable seating. If you are able to (it's OK if you are not), let the business owner know, in person or in writing, that you chose not to spend your money there because your basic needs were not accommodated. Be specific about what was lacking, using language that feels right for you.

> ### Size It Up for Yourself – Journal Entry
>
> *(continued)*
> - Get involved with a group that advocates for changes that support the improvement of living conditions for large people. If you can't find one that you like, consider starting one yourself. The Internet now makes it possible for us to easily connect with people—locally, regionally, and internationally—who we might not otherwise have access to for mutual support.
>
> Whatever you decide to do—or even if you decide to do nothing—believing that it is your basic human right to have your size-related needs accommodated will likely help you to recognize the times when they are not as an injustice—rather than believing that something is wrong with you. Doesn't that alone put the air back into the room?

FOOTNOTES

1. Carrión, Angelly, "So Tell Us, Philadelphia: What's it Like to Live in a Trinity House?," *Philadelphia*, August 3, 2015, https://www.phillymag.com/property/2015/08/03/philadelphia-trinity-homes/.

Casper, Amanda. "Row Houses," Encyclopedia of Greater Philadelphia, Rutgers University, accessed October 10, 2019, https://philadelphiaencyclopedia.org/archive/row-houses/.

2. There are some exceptions to this rule; most notably are Hawaiian and Southwest Airlines' policies for accommodating large passengers. For a comprehensive listing of airlines that have policies that address size-related accommodations visit https://www.chubbydiaries.com/post/will-your-airline-make-you-buy-an-extra-seat-on-the-plane-list-of-airlines-chubby-people-policies.

3. "Information for Operators," Federal Aviation Administration, U.S. Department of Transportation, July 30, 2012, https://www.faa.gov/other_visit/aviation_industry/airline_operators/airline_safety/info/all_infos/media/2012/info12012.pdf.

4. United States Department of Transportation, National Highway Traffic Safety Administration, Seat Belts, accessed on December 3, 2022, https://nhtsa.gov/risky-driving/seat-belts.

5. Federal Register, "Federal Motor Vehicles Safety Standards; Occupant Crash Protection, Seat Belt Assemblies," *Federal Register*, no. 03-1134 (January 2003); 2480 – 3, https://www.federalregister.gov/documents/2003/01/17/03-1134/federal-motor-vehicles-safety-standards-occupant-crash-protection-seat-belt-assemblies.

6. "The History of the Americans with Disabilities Act: A Movement Perspective," Publications, Disability Rights Education & Defense Fund, 1992, https://dredf.org/about-us/publications/the-history-of-the-ada/.

CHAPTER NINE

◆

I HAVE THE RIGHT TO MAKE LIFESTYLE CHANGES TO IMPROVE MY HEALTH AND WELL-BEING WHILE MAINTAINING A LOVING AND ACCEPTING ATTITUDE TOWARD MYSELF AND MY BODY AS I AM TODAY, WITHOUT THE NEED TO ADOPT AN ATTITUDE OF SELF- OR BODY LOATHING.

◆

CONTENT WARNING: *This chapter contains the word* ob*sity.

This is a tough one (for me, at least). In American culture, we have been socialized to celebrate the aesthetic changes that come with weight loss. ("She looks GREAT!") This cultural norm perpetuates the idea that a thin body is necessarily more attractive and appealing than a large body. The reality is that BEAUTY COMES IN ALL SHAPES AND SIZES; however, it is often difficult for large women to feel beautiful, especially when we are in the process of making lifestyle changes to support our good health and well-being. It stands to reason that if we buy into the idea that being thinner means being more attractive, then we are likely to believe that unless and until we become thin, we will not be attractive.

This can create an emotional conflict for many of us, which we may or may not be aware of. It might sound something like this: if I truly love, accept, and appreciate my body as it is now, then why would I make lifestyle changes that will probably result in at least some weight loss? Wouldn't that mean that I never truly loved, accepted, and appreciated my body?

It can be difficult to separate out making lifestyle changes to support our health and well-being from making lifestyle changes to lose weight so that we feel more socially acceptable. It took years for me to untangle my natural love of movement (exercise, dance, and, dare I say—sex?) for its own sake, from decades of linking it to weight loss. It was so bad that if I went out for a vigorous walk without my heart rate monitor (which also tracked the number of calories that I was burning), I felt like the walk did not "count." This often meant that, not only did it not count toward my efforts to lose weight, but it also didn't count as an enjoyable activity that made me feel alive and connected to the beauty of the world around me. Because my primary focus was on tracking calories burned, everything good and life-giving about these walks was lost. I am aware now that underneath it all was the belief that it was only by achieving cis-sized normativity[1] would I be truly deserving of the good things in life.

In 2014, my relationship with food and exercise became further complicated when I was diagnosed with Type II diabetes. Decades before, after years of dieting and having my food choices policed by my family and others, I made a pact with myself that I would NEVER go on another diet or allow anyone to tell me what I should or should not eat. My one exception had been: if I ever develop a life-threatening health condition and a qualified medical professional advises me to modify my diet to improve my health. Well . . . here I am. I now have a health mandate that says that losing five to ten percent of my body weight could significantly reduce my risk of developing many of the life-threatening complications of diabetes.[2] And every day I am confronted with the feeling that some *thing* (diabetes, in this case) is telling me what I should or should not be eating or drinking (I am a proud lover of sugar-sweetened beverages). And I do not believe that it is an exaggeration to say that it has been re-traumatizing. I find myself engaging in behaviors that I had stopped the moment that I decided to start making my own food choices: hiding the fact that I am consuming certain foods and beverages from people who know that I have diabetes; overeating and over-consuming beverages; and, perhaps worst of all, making food choices that are based on a deeply rooted fear of re-experiencing the terrorizing feelings of hunger and deprivation that I felt during my dieting years. Yep, that's trauma. So, my work, on this leg of my journey, is to begin to think about my healthy food choices as **empowered** choices made by someone who enjoys being healthy and despises even the mild symptoms of uncontrolled blood sugar . . . and to recognize that my days of experiencing food tyranny are OVER.

If you, too, have hurdles that you need to clear in order to be healthy and well, I believe that we can get there by offering ourselves an unending supply of **compassion**. Compassion allows us to forgive ourselves for the times that we were harsh and judgmental with ourselves. It creates space to pick ourselves up when we fall down. It allows us to feel the love for ourselves and our bodies that we have been longing for.

Is Losing Weight an Act of Treason?

Around the time that the size acceptance movement began to gain visibility (mostly on daytime talk shows in the 1980s), a debate raged among members of the movement about whether size acceptance meant that you had to love being a large (fat) person. Like in most movements, the most radical members believed that it did, and they routinely handed out indictments of anyone who did not, insisting that they were not truly accepting of their bodies. A couple of decades later, I remember Queen Latifah, iconic rapper, actor, producer, and talk show host, making a statement of solidarity with "big girls" after she had lost a significant amount of weight. While it was heartwarming, it seemed to give legitimacy to the idea that going from being a large person to being a cis-sized person is, in fact, a betrayal to the size acceptance movement. It begs the question: is losing weight an act of treason to the size acceptance movement?

For me, size acceptance, body positivity, and size equity have more to do with a fundamental belief that we all have the right to feel good about our bodies, to live free from size-related discrimination, and to live full and satisfying lives. Period. A size equity perspective supports an idea that you will see throughout this book: that **ALL BODIES ARE GOOD**

BODIES. There is no more inherent value in large bodies than there is in cis-sized bodies. In female and non-binary bodies than in male bodies. In the bodies of people of color than in white bodies. In the bodies of members of the various religious and spiritual groups throughout the world than in Christian bodies. In the bodies of people who live in poverty than in the bodies of those who have access to wealth. In lesbian, gay, bisexual, and queer bodies than in heterosexual bodies. In transgender and intersex bodies than in cis-gendered bodies. In old bodies than in young bodies. In disabled bodies than in abled bodies. All bodies are good bodies. And we all have the right to make lifestyle changes that positively affect our health and well-being—even if these changes lead to weight loss.

Size It Up for Yourself – Journal Entry

- Do you currently have concerns related to your health and well-being that you would like to address?
- What has been your experience around making lifestyle changes to improve your health and well-being?
- What have been your successes?
- Where have you struggled, or been unable to accomplish the changes that you desire?
- Where can you begin to infuse some **compassion** for yourself where you have been harsh or judgmental? (Hint: diet talk is the opposite of compassion.)
- What are some healthy ways that you can reward yourself for your progress?

If you believe that it would be helpful, consider using this chart to track your experience around making lifestyle changes. See the Appendix for a blank copy of this chart.

Health/Wellness CONCERN:	Barriers to Improvement:	Compassionate Solutions:	Healthy Rewards:	Process Notes:
(example): Type II diabetes	my trauma around my history of food restriction	• remind myself that I, alone, am in control of my choices, and that this is different from when others policed my choices • attend therapy to continue the work of processing and healing my trauma	• mani/pedis • massages • visit an art gallery	I am noticing that, when I think of my choices as my own, there are times when I actually crave water. In the past, I associated water with restriction and deprivation, so I thought that I hated it.

TABLE 9.1: Healthy Lifestyle Changes Tracking Chart

Please also consider the fact that **health** and **weight** are two separate issues—though we almost always lump them together in our culture. A person can choose to commit themselves to a healthy lifestyle without necessarily being concerned with losing weight. Two examples of this idea are the Health at Every Size (HAES) movement and intuitive eating.[3] Of course, for some people who improve, for example, the nutritional content of the food that they eat, weight loss will be an outcome. Some argue that the medical community does not have conclusive evidence that obesity alone is a significant risk factor for many diseases.[4] What seems clear, however, is that many chronic health conditions can be improved for many large people if they engage in activities and make dietary choices that may result in losing a certain percentage of their body weight. For many people who suffer from chronic health conditions (like me), this is a compelling argument for adopting new, healthier, eating and movement behaviors. However, this does not mean that we must abandon our body love and acceptance and adopt an angry, hate-filled, shameful, punitive attitude toward our bodies.

A Word About Weight Loss Surgery

In the past decade or so, bariatric surgery has gained ever-increasing popularity as a method of weight loss. The most commonly performed procedure, the Laparoscopic Roux-en-Y Gastric Bypass, is the descendent of procedures that were performed as far back as the 1960s, and appears to be much safer than its predecessors.[5] However, this section is not about the pros and cons of weight loss surgery. It is, instead, about an individual's unequivocal right to choose to have it. Over the years, I have heard the judgmental whispers of some large folks about other large folks who have "had the surgery." Most of the whispers have been about aesthetic outcomes: "She looks much older," or, "His skin is hanging." I suspect that these judgments are rooted in something less superficial than they might seem. At least two things might be happening: first, I wonder if some of the whisperers, having internalized negative beliefs about their own large bodies, are unconsciously (or consciously, in some cases) feeling jealous or competitive toward the weight losers; second, I wonder if there is a subtle grief experience occurring. That is to say, this person—who can no longer be described as a large person—is no longer able to share in the experience of what it is like to live in a size-bigoted world *in real time*, experiencing and responding to the everyday insults that are lurking at every turn.

There is a scene in the movie *The Mirror Has Two Faces*[6] that illustrates this perfectly. Rose Morgan, played by Barbara Streisand, is a Humanities professor at an Ivy League university. Having previously balked at many of the things that women do in the name of beauty (for example, wearing makeup, counting calories, etc.), Rose decides to "improve" her appearance, losing some weight and updating her look, in the hopes of seducing a man (insert eye roll here). In one scene, she is having lunch with one of her friends, Doris, a woman who is to the right of cis-sized and has been Rose's comrade in quietly protesting the absurd expectations that have been put on women in our society. Doris begins to lament the fact that she now feels alone in the struggle:

Doris: "I just thought we'd always be in the same boat, ya' know what I'm sayin'? Made it easier somehow."

Rose: (nodding sympathetically) "I know."

Even if you've never seen the movie, this brief snippet of dialogue gives you a sense of how deeply impacted Doris is by the loss of having Rose as someone who is walking the same walk that she is. Can you relate? This is grief. And it is the grief that needs to be addressed rather than further marginalizing individuals who have made a choice that is right for them. For some people, weight loss surgery has been a life-saving choice. It is also the marginalization of large people, in general, that needs to be addressed. Because it is the loneliness of not feeling like an accepted member of society that makes finding community among other large people necessary, and that makes losing a member of the group so painful.

FOOTNOTES

1. See Glossary for a definition of cis-size normativity.

2. U.S. Department of Health & Human Services, Centers for Disease Control and Prevention, Diabetes: Healthy Weight, last reviewed April 28, 2021, https://cdc.gov/diabetes/managing/healthy-weight.html.

3. Because of my own trauma around dieting, and because I am sensitive to the experiences of other large women who have been traumatized by—or just inundated with—negative messages, internal and external, about their relationship with food and eating, I will not endorse any program or plan that involves modifying one's behaviors around food and eating. This book is about empowering women to make their own choices about how they live. If you would like more information about HAES or intuitive eating, the Internet is a great resource.

4. "Obesity Alone Does Not Increase Risk of Death: New Study Could Change the Way We Think About Obesity and Health," York University (website), Science Daily, July 12, 2018, www.sciencedaily.com/releases/2018/07/180712114440.htm.

5. Faria, Gil R., "A Brief History of Bariatric Surgery," *Porto Biomedical Journal 2*, no. 3 (May – June 2017): 90-2, https://www.sciencedirect.com/science/article/pii/S2444866416300186 on April 23, 2018.

6. Streisand, Barbra, director. *The Mirror Has Two Faces*. 1996; Culver City, CA: TriStar Pictures.

CHAPTER TEN

◆

I HAVE THE RIGHT TO MAKE MY OWN DECISIONS ABOUT HOW I WILL MANAGE MY HEALTH (INCLUDING MY FOOD CHOICES). NO ONE, INCLUDING MY HEALTH CARE PROVIDERS AND FITNESS CONSULTANTS, HAS THE RIGHT TO BULLY ME ABOUT MY CHOICES BY ARGUING THAT THEY ARE CONCERNED ABOUT MY HEALTH.

◆

The issue of health might very well be the most controversial issue that has been taken up by the size acceptance movement. There are those who say that the size acceptance movement is just an excuse for large people to continue their bad habits around food, eating, and exercise, and to not take responsibility for their own health and wellness. There are others, like the Health at Every Size (HAES) movement, who ". . . promote size-acceptance, to end weight discrimination, and to lessen the cultural obsession with weight loss and thinness. [They] promote . . . balanced eating, life-enhancing physical activity, and respect for the diversity of body shapes and sizes."[1]

I am of the belief that health (or the lack of it) is a personal choice.

I just felt the muscles of every person reading this tighten, and every eyebrow raise. In fact, as I type this, it feels like a radical idea to me. As a culture, health is a value that we hold in high esteem—even if our individual behaviors fall short of supporting our good health. We render judgment on people who regularly engage in habits like smoking, drinking to excess, overeating, or consuming foods with high fat, salt, or sugar content (these last two are mostly reserved for large folks). Health, or the lack of it, becomes a matter for public scrutiny.

Our bodies, and how we live in them, are no one else's concern but our own. As a social worker, I am a staunch advocate of the principle of self-determination.[2] This principle becomes complicated when we think about the impact of poor health on relationships and on public and private resources. However, I hold true to the belief that, unless we are personally responsible for managing the consequences of a person's poor health, their health is none of our concern. And even then, there are limitations to what we have a say about. Every person has the right to make their own decisions about how they will manage their health.

The belief that other people have a say about how we manage our health has been a costly one—for women in particular, and for large women, especially. In addition to the social pressure that we experience to be thin—**at any cost**—so that we *look* acceptable, so many of us, at one time or another, have modified our eating and exercise habits because others have expressed concern about our health. Many of these modifications have been detrimental to our physical and mental health: starvation, restrictive eating, binging and purging, over-exercising, and other types of disordered eating and exercise habits. Ironically, after all the years I spent engaging in some of these unhealthy behaviors trying (unsuccessfully) to lose weight, I now weigh about fifty pounds less than I did before. I shifted my focus to (a) moving in ways that support my aging body; and (b) trying to make food choices that help me to manage my Type II diabetes. Losing weight is now the furthest thing from my mind.

Furthermore, there is no conclusive medical evidence that all occurrences of any particular illness or disease (e.g., hypertension, diabetes) are the result of lifestyle choices. And people of all sizes have been diagnosed with health conditions that our society (and the medical establishment) typically associate with large bodies. The research that attempts to provide evidence of a causal link between size and the development of many health conditions has only been able to conclude that a person's weight **may** put them at increased risk for certain health conditions.[3] Moreover, we know that *risk factors are not the same as causes*. And other factors, like heredity, also play a role in determining our degree of risk.

The Policing of Our Food Choices

One of the primary ways that other people insert themselves into how we manage our health is by policing our food choices. This practice has become so acceptable in our culture that it is almost an automatic response for most people to routinely notice what a large person is eating. And, along with the noticing, comes a silent (or loud) judgment about whether our choices are "appropriate." What a burden we carry. Food is essential to our survival. But, because of this constant surveillance, many of us do not know what it is like to eat ANYTHING without evaluating it—and ourselves—as "good" or "bad." The idea of food for food's sake is a foreign concept. Rather than trusting our natural, instinctual appetites to inform us about what our body needs or wants, many of us have developed a distorted way of relating to food that casts it as both an evil siren beckoning us to our demise *and* as a faithful friend who is a reliable source of comfort and pleasure.

Size It Up for Yourself – Journal Entry

(Reclaiming Your Right to Eat)
If your relationship with food and eating causes you distress *in any way*, I invite you to think about how you can reclaim your right to eat without the burden of judgment. It might be helpful to spend some time exploring some of these questions in your journal:
- What has been your experience around food and eating? Your attitudes and behaviors might have changed over time, so it might be helpful to track them chronologically.
- Can you remember any times when you ate something without judging yourself, positively or negatively, or without fearing judgment or seeking approval from others? If so, can you use that experience as a reminder that it is OK not to judge yourself about what

> ### Size It Up for Yourself – Journal Entry
>
> *(continued)* you eat all the time? If you cannot remember a time, might it be exciting to think about experimenting with not judging yourself or internalizing the judgments of others?
> - How do you want to manage the feeling that other people are monitoring what you eat? For example, do you want to remind yourself about your right to eat whatever you want, whenever you want? When I started doing this, I noticed that I began to make my food choices based on what I was craving rather than (a) going for the gold star by eating a salad (no croutons or dressing, please) when I wanted a burger; or (b) making choices that were not what I really wanted—as an act of defiance, or to avoid feeling deprived. Trusting my natural instincts and appetites about what (and how much) to eat has allowed me to enjoy food without shame and regret and to eliminate virtually all of the gastrointestinal distress that I experienced from forcing things into my body that it did not want.
> - How do you want to respond to others who openly police your food choices? Do you want to call out the inappropriateness of their remarks, giving them a dose of healthy shame (there is such a thing)? Whatever you decide to do, do it in the name of honoring the sovereignty that you have with your own body.

Health Policing AKA Bullying

Large women are often bullied about lifestyle choices that have the potential to impact our health. These bullying behaviors frequently come from others who claim to be motivated by concern. Experience, and listening to the accounts of other large women, have led me to believe that these concerns are very rarely legitimate. More often they are passive-aggressive (perhaps even unconscious, at times) attempts to degrade us in order for the other person to assert a sense of superiority. In what other context do we believe that it is OK for one adult to have a say about another adult's choices? This is usually only thought of as warranted if a person is impaired in some way (e.g., if an adult has moderate to severe intellectual disabilities). Otherwise, it is paternalistic, condescending, and insulting.

Unfortunately, health care providers and fitness professionals are some of the biggest perpetrators of this kind of insult. Because they are in the business of advising people about their health, some (many?) of them believe that this gives them license to disregard the social conventions around treating people with dignity and respect. I know from my own experiences in recent years that it is possible to give health advice without being paternalistic, condescending, or insulting. There are health care providers and fitness professionals out there who value relating to their large patients and clients in ways that respect them as consumers, but first and foremost, as people. For the sake of our own wellness, these are the health care professionals worth finding. Chapter 13 has suggestions for questions that you might ask when you are screening a new health care provider.

FOOTNOTES

1. "HAES® Approach," Association for Size Diversity and Health (ASDAH), accessed June 19, 2018, https://www.sizediversityandhealth.org/.

2. See Glossary for a definition of the principle of self-determination.

3. U.S. Department of Health & Human Services, The National Institute of Diabetes and Digestive and Kidney Diseases Health Information Center, Health Risks of Overweight & Obesity, Last reviewed February2018, https://www.niddk.nih.gov/health-information/weight-management/health-risks-overweight.

CHAPTER ELEVEN

I HAVE THE RIGHT TO HONOR MY BODY'S LIMITATIONS, WITHOUT SHAME OR EMBARRASSMENT.

Recently, I was reminded of how painful and enduring the scars that are left from body-shaming experiences can be. I was at my body-affirming exercise class attempting to achieve the Warrior III yoga pose. I was having difficulty holding the pose, and after wobbling for a few seconds, fell out of it completely. Now, I have heard my instructor's gentle and reassuring voice from the front of the room every . . . single . . . class giving us permission to listen to our own bodies about what they need, and to adjust the pose accordingly. I have also fallen out of Warrior III many times. But for some reason, on this particular morning, I found myself making plans in my head to practice the pose at home until I had perfected it. I suddenly flashed back to a scene from my first year of high school: I had been mortified in a middle-school PE class the year before, as I observed a cis-sized classmate imitating me attempting to tumble on a mat during an obstacle course run. She repeatedly flung herself onto the mat (as I had, moments before) while she and some other students laughed hysterically.

When the time came during my freshmen year of high school to tumble on the mat as part of the annual physical fitness test, I resolved to spare myself the same humiliation. For weeks I dragged two twin-sized mattresses downstairs to the living room, lined them up end-to-end to create a makeshift gym mat, and attempted to tumble. Despite my fervent efforts, I was never able to will my body to flip over itself. The message that I took away from this, and other experiences like it, was that my body was not competent around movement, and that this was directly related to the size of my body. As a result, I have often felt the need to push my body past its limits.

When surrounded by cis-sized people, I used to feel the need to keep up with their pace—walking, climbing stairs, dancing, cleaning—whatever. In fact, just recently, I lapsed back into this old behavior while I was at the beach with two of my cis-sized friends. Now, I could not ask for two more supportive allies in my journey around size acceptance. But on this day, I was feeling the old pangs of not wanting to stand out, not wanting to feel different (inferior, really), as I thought about how I would get up from my very fabulous . . . but also very low . . . beach chair. One of my friends had said earlier that her knee was swollen and that it had been bothering her. I found myself secretly hoping that she would have to struggle to get out of her chair. This was not a wish for my friend to have less mobility or to suffer in any way. It was a wish to not feel alone in my suffering. To not feel singled out in such an embarrassing way.

If our culture made space for it to be OK for *every body* to move in whatever way it needs or wants to move, then this kind of shame and embarrassment would not exist. We would take the time that we need to honor our bodies' limitations and to treat them the way that they deserve to be treated. Unfortunately, change *at the societal level* comes slowly. In the meantime, **you can make a commitment to yourself** to make it a practice to lovingly listen to your body for information about what it needs. I will take this opportunity to once again remind you that developing a practice is just that: like learning to play the piano, or acquiring any new skill, you will need to do it over and over and over again, until it becomes intuitive. You will not always hit your mark. And you might be tempted to be angry with yourself, or to abandon your practice altogether. But that is the precise moment when you can offer yourself kindness and compassion and recommit yourself to your practice in preparation for the next time that you are confronted with this issue.

> ### Size It Up for Yourself – Journal Entry
>
> - What have been some of your experiences around recognizing your body's limitations (e.g., limitations related to stamina, flexibility, movement, pain, disability, access)?
> - How can you empower yourself to honor these limitations? Here are some ideas:
>   - **Develop a mantra that reminds you that it is OK to go at your own pace.** Keep it short and simple (perhaps even catchy!) so that it will be easy to remember.
>   - **Find a tangible reminder of your intention to honor your body's limits.** For example, you might find a trinket (like a tiny turtle) to wear on a bracelet to remind yourself to slow down. This is just one example—the possibilities are endless!
>   - **Modify an activity to accommodate your body's needs**. I could have held on to the arms of my beach chair, and then pushed my body forward until my knees were in the sand, then put my hands in the sand in front of them (or swiveled around and held on to the arms of the chair), and then slowly raised myself up to a standing position. That is what my body needed.
>   - **Give yourself permission to skip an activity that will likely tax you beyond your limitations.**
>   - **Ask for help.**
>
>   Keep in mind that it is also OK to challenge yourself. If it is safe for you to push past your current limits, and you have a desire to do so, go for it!

Over thirty years after my tumbling debacle, I decided to spend one Thanksgiving holiday at a luxury hotel and spa. One of the activities that the hotel offered for guests was a Thanksgiving morning walk/run through the back woods of Pennsylvania. I participated in the walk and had been chatting with a lovely family from California when the trail began to get steeper. As my heart rate increased, I wanted to slow down, but I worried, for a moment, that the family (all of them cis-sized) would be judging me. And then I reminded myself that the whole point of this trip was to relax and enjoy myself. So, I slowed down. I enjoyed the beauty of the woods and the crisp, fall mountain air as I watched the California family disappear around a bend up ahead. Much of the trail was steep enough for me to still get a good cardio workout ***at my own pace.*** I realized that day that life is best enjoyed when we do what feels good for ourselves based on our own needs and standards.

CHAPTER TWELVE

◆

I HAVE THE RIGHT TO RESPECTFULLY
USE OR TAKE UP SPACE, AND TO BE OPEN AND
EXPANSIVE IN MY BODY, AND TO NOT FEEL THE
NEED TO COVER, HIDE, DECREASE, SHRINK
AWAY, OR OTHERWISE ATTEMPT TO APPEAR
SMALLER TO AVOID REAL OR PERCEIVED
JUDGMENT FROM OTHERS.

◆

How do you live in your body?

Because our bodies are often treated as socially unacceptable, many of us have crafted a way of being in them that are unconscious (and sometimes conscious) attempts to appear smaller—or even to feel invisible. We might avoid eye contact, the way that young children sometimes do, almost believing that, "if I can't see you, then you can't see me." Or perhaps believing that we can prevent the other person from seeing our shame if they cannot see our eyes. We might speak softly, or not at all, in public spaces. Maybe we turn down invitations to be out and about with others. These are a few of the ways that we deny ourselves full and complete access to the world outside of our bodies. Without realizing it, we become somewhat captive in our bodies, fearing that living more expansively will invite criticism and judgment from others.

Size It Up for Yourself – Avoidance Checklist

In what ways do you intentionally or unintentionally avoid taking up space or being seen by others?

____ I avoid eye contact with others.
____ I speak softly when I am in public spaces.
____ I avoid speaking altogether when I am in public spaces.
____ I avoid going places (e.g., restaurants, entertainment venues) without having other people along to act as buffers against potential harassment.
____ I turn down invitations from friends to hang out in public.
____ I hunch my shoulders.
____ I tighten my muscles.
____ I hold in my stomach.
____ My breathing is often shallow when I am around others.
____ I dissociate.
____ I always defer to others in public (e.g., letting them walk ahead of me).
____ I buy clothes that I believe will cover, hide, or camouflage the parts of my body that I do not feel good about.

____ _____
____ _____
____ _____

Now that you have begun the work of becoming aware of the ways that you have been diminishing yourself to avoid the pain of being judged by others, how do you feel about it? If you are like me, then you probably feel cheated. Think about all the experiences that we have been missing out on by hiding inside of our bodies. What will you do when you no longer feel the need to do this? Will you fully extend your arms upward in moments of celebration (or gratitude, or praise)? Will you wear something that you love, even though it reveals a part of your body that you have been trying to hide? Will you allow yourself to feel the pleasure of relaxing your body from head to toe? Better yet: will you find a size-affirming massage therapist to usher you into a state of pure relaxation? The sky's the limit!

After years of covering and hiding ourselves, it is unlikely that these old behaviors will just fall away. For most of us, it will take time to unlearn the strategies that we have developed to help us to feel safer in the world. And thank goodness we had them! Otherwise, we would have been defenseless against the pain that comes from the poor treatment that we often experience as large people. In my work with my clients, I love to use the language of "experimenting" with new behaviors. This lens allows us to let go of the expectation of a particular outcome. We are free to be curious and to just observe what unfolds. If we think of each experiment as providing us with information that will help us to move closer to our ultimate goal—feeling free to respectfully take up space in the world and live openly and expansively in our bodies—then we will likely have more emotional capacity for tolerating experiences (experiments) that do not go the way that we want them to. They become just one more source of information for us.

Size It Up for Yourself – Experimenting with New Behaviors

Here is an example to help you to get in the frame of mind of **experimenting** with new behaviors:

Imagine going to the park alone, and shortly after finding a comfortable seat on a bench, you **observe** some people staring at you. Here are some examples of how you might respond:

- You might consider the possibility that they are staring at you for reasons other than your body size. How do you think you might feel if you believed that this is a possibility? Would it be enough to allow you to relax and enjoy your time in the park?
- If you are fairly certain that people are staring at you because of your size, you still have options for how you might respond:
  - You might decide to have a conversation with yourself that allows you to **externalize** the behavior, e.g., by telling yourself: "this person has a narrow, oppressive view of bodies. They are not aware that while they are judging me, they are also putting limitations on the circumstances under which they can feel good about their

Size It Up for Yourself – Experimenting with New Behaviors

(continued) own body. I choose not to participate in this kind of oppressive thinking. I choose to feel good about my body and to be accepting of other people's bodies." In this example, the focus is shifted to the other person's behavior **(external)** rather than believing that the stares are confirmation that there is something wrong with you **(internal)**. **What are some other conversations that you could have with yourself?** _____

_____

_____

_____

- You might consider finding a way to confront the behavior. I recently saw a social media post that was a photograph of a woman with the words "FUCK YOU" written on her ample double chin. I thought that it was badass—and I silently celebrated her—but I was also aware that she will likely receive hateful responses from people who are always poised to try to tear others down. If you believe that you would be mostly unharmed by the negative responses that you might get from this kind of protest, I say, go for it! There are also less provocative[1] ways of confronting bad behavior. For example, what do you think it would be like to make eye contact with the person who is staring, and to smile (or not) and say, "Hello"? My thought is that this response might (a) disarm the person; and (b) cause them to be more sensitive to the fact that you are a human being just as they are, and that their behavior has an impact on you. When we retreat into ourselves, we are inadvertently sending the message that the other person does not have to be accountable for their behavior. And we carry their shame instead of handing it back to them. **How might you directly or indirectly confront negative behavior directed at you from others because of your size?**
- **If at the end of this experiment you do not feel any better, what information can you use from it to improve your experience the next time that you are in this situation?**

Making Ourselves Smaller

Sometime during my pre-adolescent years, my mother taught me that I should hold my stomach in whenever I was out in public. In her world, there was no room for stomachs that were not completely flat. When I became a full-fledged adolescent, she made me wear the dreaded "panty girdle" under my clothes on special occasions. It was tantamount to a medieval torture device! However, over time, holding my stomach in became as automatic as breathing. A couple of decades into my size-affirming life, I realized that I was still doing it. Not only was I still doing it, but I noticed that my baseline level of anxiety was higher when I was doing it. This makes sense when we consider what was happening in my body. Our bodies are designed to detect danger, and then to cue our nervous system to activate the fight-flight-freeze response. This response includes, among other things, tightening of the muscles. When we tighten our muscles in the absence of threat, we send our brains the false signal that there is danger present, and our anxiety naturally goes up. I also believe that holding in our stomachs sends the message—to ourselves—that we are not OK just as we are.

This is not an argument against shapewear, or even holding in one's stomach for that matter. The point here is that there is nothing inherently wrong with the size and shape of our bodies and, therefore, we have the right to forgo such practices—if we choose—and to live in our bodies fully and expansively. This includes resisting the urge to use clothes to cover the parts of our bodies that we deem unacceptable. It means sitting in the front of the class instead of hiding out in the back . . . and not squeezing ourselves into spaces that do not fit our beautiful bodies. It means letting our voices be heard. We have a lot to say.

FOOTNOTES

1. I am aware that referring to some behaviors that are meant to call out injustice as "provocative" sounds a bit like victim-blaming. I want to be clear: I believe that people have the right to make whatever statements they wish about injustice without receiving harmful or abusive backlash. My use of the word provocative is purely semantic: the protest behavior leads to but does

not cause the harmful or abusive response. The responsibility always lies with the perpetrator of hateful acts and remarks for making them.

CHAPTER THIRTEEN

I HAVE THE RIGHT TO QUALITY HEALTH CARE FROM HEALTH CARE PROVIDERS WHO TREAT ME WITH DIGNITY AND RESPECT, TAKE MY SYMPTOMS SERIOUSLY, AND ENGAGE IN THOROUGH ASSESSMENT AND TREATMENT PRACTICES THAT ARE FREE FROM SIZE-RELATED BIAS.

CONTENT WARNING: *This chapter contains the word* ob*sity.

When I was younger, I blamed and shamed myself when I got poor treatment from doctors because of their assumptions about my health based upon my weight. Before I started choosing my own health care providers, I found myself filled with dread when I had to go to see a doctor. I came to believe that whatever symptoms I had were the direct result of my size. I would almost rather have continued to suffer with whatever ailment I had than to have experienced the soul-crushing shame of being told by yet another arrogant, judgmental doctor to simply "lose weight." I came across this cartoon online that captures my experience perfectly:

Image courtesy of Stephen Taaffe @bogswallop

I was very healthy during my childhood, adolescence, and early adulthood. Except for the common childhood illnesses, most of my visits to the doctor's office were for annual wellness checks, and I was always given a clean bill of health. However, many of those visits concluded with me or my mother being handed that dreaded printout of a nutritional chart, with a heavy emphasis on calories, and a recommended daily caloric intake for me, circled by the doctor. No one ever seemed concerned about how much Vitamin C I was getting!

At no time during those years was I ever asked about other factors that contribute to (or detract from) good health, like my activity level, my experience in my family and my community, or even my ACTUAL eating habits. My parents were both raised on farms, so our family diet was very well-balanced. But my doctors' assessments were strictly one-dimensional—based on the numbers that they saw on the scale. In hindsight, I believe that this experience (along with others) was a major contributing factor to my spending my late childhood and my ENTIRE adolescence obsessed with losing weight rather than just enjoying my life. What a loss. What else might I have been doing, and in what ways might I have flourished, if so much of my mental, emotional, physical, and psychological energy had not been bogged down with searching for the perfect weight loss solution? If you have had a similar experience, you owe it to yourself to reclaim those lost parts of yourself.

Rebecca Stritchfield, dietician, exercise physiologist, and author of the book *Body Kindness,* wrote a thoughtful piece about how things might be different for large patients if body weight was not the gold standard that physicians use to assess health and to make health care recommendations.[1] She reviewed studies that found that the stigma, shame, and stress that many large patients have experienced during doctor visits increases the likelihood that they will stop seeing a doctor altogether, putting them at a higher risk for developing health conditions that go undetected, and therefore untreated. Until recently, I used to (somewhat) obsessively watch reality shows about weight loss—partly because they provided me with validation about what it feels like to be a large person in the world, and partly because they gave me hope of one day losing enough weight to feel completely OK with myself. As a side note, I can now say—triumphantly—that I no longer feel the need to lose weight in order to feel whole. It took forty-two years for me to get to this place. Writing this book is probably what ultimately got me here. It is my great hope that using this book will help you to get where you want to be—and in a lot less time. In recent years, I have been particularly drawn to TLC's *My 600-lb. Life*. However, the last time that I watched it, I was so disgusted by the way that the show's bariatric surgeon, Dr. Younan Nowzaradan, spoke to his patient about weight loss plateaus that I don't know if I will ever watch the show again.[2]

It was not the first time that I noticed "Dr. Now's" insensitive, demeaning, paternalistic way of relating to his patients when they are struggling, but this time, it was really upsetting to think about the gravity of the implications of what he was doing. On this episode, he said, about a woman who had lost some weight but whose weight loss had stalled, that if she did not have a significant reduction in her weight by the next office visit, there was little hope that she would ever lose the weight. I suspect that these kinds of declarations are made for dramatic effect—which might make for good TV—but WHY IN THE WORLD would a medical professional *ever* make such a dire prediction about someone's life?! *And* put it out into the Universe for others to potentially believe? And based on what evidence? I know that, as viewers, we are only privy to snapshots of these folks' journeys. But in what we are permitted to see, there is no compassion—only accusations based on logic about "calories in and calories out." There is very little attention given to the emotional and psychological (or medical, for that matter) factors that impact a person's ability to lose weight and maintain the weight loss. How irresponsible. This is nothing more than size shaming hiding under the guise of sound medical care.

There are studies now emerging that show that, if a health care provider has negative attitudes about large people, the quality of care that they provide may be substandard.[3] For example, they might spend less time with a large patient, believing that the visit is a waste of time because the patient is unlikely to follow their recommendations. They might be less likely to order diagnostic tests, defaulting to the assumption that the problem is weight related. Some surgeons will not perform knee and hip replacements on large people, and size is not always factored in when determining medication doses (i.e. a large body might need a higher dose of a medication in order for it to be effective). At the institutional level, many medical facilities are not equipped with scales and diagnostic instruments (like MRI scanners) that can accommodate people above a certain weight.

We all, regardless of our size, deserve to have our health care needs addressed in an environment that feels safe (i.e. free from size-related bias), and with providers who care about the quality of the services that they provide to **everyone**. We deserve providers who respond to us in ways that communicate that they value us and are committed to working toward the best possible outcomes. If this is not your current experience with *all* of your health care providers, here are some suggestions for helping you to get the care that you deserve:

- **Change providers.** If you encounter a health care provider who treats you disrespectfully, dismisses your concerns, or **in any other way** makes you feel unsafe or uncomfortable, consider changing providers. If you would like to offer corrective feedback to the provider or the facility that employs them, by all means do. However, in most cases, I would not recommend that you continue receiving care from this provider. Negative biases are deeply embedded in the minds (and sometimes, hearts) of people who hold them, and they are unlikely to improve without a lot of soul-searching and a deep commitment to change.
- **Don't be afraid to ask questions.** Whether you have a

long-standing relationship with a trusted primary care provider, are visiting a specialist, or are seeing a new provider for the first time, you have the right to have all your questions about your health care answered. ***It is never too late to start asking for what you need.*** This also applies to visits with allied providers such as physical and occupational therapists, mental health providers, nutritionists, and in-home health care providers. Here are some questions that you might want to ask with new providers:

- Does your facility have the equipment and resources to accommodate my size-related needs? If not, do you have access to or privileges at other facilities that do?
- What are your attitudes, beliefs, and methods for treating patients with a body mass index (BMI) of thirty or above?
- Can I count on you to do a thorough assessment of my health care needs and not default to believing that my concerns are size/weight-related?
- **Stand up for yourself.** If, without medical evidence, your health care provider directly (or indirectly) indicates that they believe that your health concern is the result of your size, Ragen Chastain, a speaker, writer, and thought leader in the areas of weight stigma and weight-inclusive healthcare and fitness, suggests, among other things, that you use the following phrases to communicate with them about your care:
    - "Do thin people get this health problem? What do you recommend for them?"
    - "Please provide me with evidence-based [medical care] and the opportunity for informed consent." (I especially like this one. Doctors are always trying to avoid malpractice lawsuits, so the use of some legal language will likely keep them on their toes!)
    - "In the limited amount of time that we have, I'd like to focus on what I came in for."[4]

I would also suggest that you ask your provider to explain things that you do not understand to you until it makes sense.

Taking Care of Ourselves

As I mentioned earlier, some studies show that if a person believes that they are going to be treated poorly by a health care provider, they are more likely to avoid medical visits. And, as I stated at the beginning of this chapter, I have been one of those people. And, as much as I understand what it feels like to walk into a potentially humiliating situation, I also believe that we surrender our personal power when we do not take care of ourselves for fear of how we will be treated. I do not want to imply that this is easy. But I do believe that the more that we advocate for ourselves—and each other—the easier it will become. This requires us to adopt the attitude that ANY poor treatment is unacceptable, and to make noise about it. And if we need support in finding our voices, we can partner with allies who can make noise for and with us. This might mean taking a support person with you to your doctor's visit. It is *THAT* important. You are *THAT* important.

Telling Our Stories

Some years ago, I attended a women's health conference that is held annually at one of the megachurches in my neighborhood. I was feeling really good about the morning workshops that I had attended and, in general, was feeling proud of myself for being there despite my history of health care being a source of anxiety and shame. The keynote speaker for the conference was a Black OB/GYN who, unbeknownst to me at the time, was somewhat of a rock star in the community. I had attended and enjoyed one of her workshops earlier in the day, so I was excited to hear her keynote address. It was fantastic! At the end of her talk, she opened the floor of the massive auditorium, full of women of all ages, shapes, and sizes for questions about sexual health. I had been wanting an answer to a particular question for some time and had received a sex-shaming, uninformative reply from a doctor in my primary care doctor's office. So, I boldly (but not without anxiety) raised my hand. I was handed the microphone and, with all the confidence that I could muster, I stood up and asked my question: given the fact that hormone-based contraception puts large women at an increased risk for having a stroke, can you recommend some non-hormonal options for birth control besides condoms? Deep exhale. Now I could relax and get the information that I had been wanting. She gave some options (none of which I can remember now) and then paused, leaning on her pulpit, looked directly at me, and said into her microphone for all to hear, "but you know that you need to lose the weight, right?" Even writing this just now, I had to take my hands away from the keyboard and just hold my face in them as the feelings of embarrassment, shame, and demoralization came flooding back and washed over me.

Luckily, I was with a (cis-sized) friend who was sensitive to the sting of the remark, and she offered me immediate, tactfully delivered, comfort. The moral of this story, for me, is that there is a culture that exists among health care providers that suggests that they are duty-bound to deliver the message about the perils of "obesity" whenever and wherever an opportunity presents itself . . . by any means necessary. This was a talk about sexual health. As far as I am concerned, the scope of her remarks should have been limited to offering information about sexual health. My question itself provided proof that I was aware of the weight-related health risks of some forms of contraception (a sexual health topic). Her comment also speaks to a certain entitlement that (some) health care providers feel about ordering—as opposed to recommending—their patients to follow their recommendations. It is very paternalistic. And quite different from how I, as a therapist, was trained. One of the core values of my profession is self-determination, which charges social workers to "respect and promote" the right of every individual and group to make their own decisions about their lives.[5] This value is also captured in the tenth amendment of *The Large Person's Bill of Rights*.

Size It Up for Yourself – Journal Entry

Telling our stories with **_compassion_**, **_concern_**, _and_ **_curiosity_**—to ourselves and to others who support us—provides us with great opportunities for healing and goes a long way toward banishing the toxic shame that we often carry as a result of how we are sometimes treated by health care professionals.

- What have been some of the negative experiences (e.g., poor quality of care; providers who were disrespectful and whose behavior caused you to feel embarrassed, humiliated, or ashamed) that you have had with health care providers? **[Concern]**
- What negative beliefs (if any) did you internalize about yourself as a result of these experiences? **[Curiosity]**
- How can you let go of (or transform) those beliefs in ways that allow you to believe positive things about yourself? **[Compassion]** This might feel especially difficult to do. One reason for this is that, as a society, we have given doctors a LOT of power and authority. They have knowledge and skills that can literally save our lives; however, this power and authority needs to be balanced with the reality that they use their expertise _in a service capacity_. Which means that, whether they choose to believe it or not, they have a moral and ethical obligation to engage in practices that do not cause harm to their patients in any way. For if, in the course of healing a broken leg, your words, attitudes, and assumptions lead to a broken spirit, then are you really engaged in the business of healing? As a woman who has likely spent a lifetime deferring to your health care providers, it might require some effort to shift to the perspective of seeing yourself as a consumer of services. As such, _your provider works for you._ You get to call the shots.

CHAPTER THIRTEEN

FOOTNOTES

CONTENT WARNING: *This footnote contains the word ob*sity.*

1. The U.S. Prevention Task Force recommends the following screenings for obesity: (a) taking a patient's weight; (b) calculating a patient's body mass index (BMI); and (c) providing or referring patients with a BMI of thirty or higher for "intensive behavioral interventions"

Stritchfield, Rebecca. What if Physicians Stopped Weighing Heavier Patients? Health Care Might Improve," Wellness, Washington Post, June 20, 2018, https://www.washingtonpost.com/lifestyle/home/what-if-physicians-stopped-weighing-0/heavier-patients-health-care-might-improve/2018/06/18/3e-b32ae4-635c-11e8-a768-ed043e33f1dc_story.html.

2. During the coronavirus (COVID-19) pandemic, I have been watching a lot more television than usual. After exhausting most of the shows that are related to topics that I find interesting and entertaining, I, apprehensively, resorted to watching *My 600-lb. Life* again. For the most part, my observations about Dr. Nowzaradan's interactions with patients holds up. However, I want to be fair by acknowledging that (a) there are times when he refers patients to psychotherapy to help them to address emotional and psychological issues that might be creating barriers for them to losing weight; and (b) I was extremely impressed by the empathy that he showed the family after the patient died before the end of treatment in the episode "Robert's Story," (Nowzaradan and McAnally 2018) and the statements that he made in the wake of Robert's death about the ways that the health care system fails patients who are in the 600+-lb. range (01:20:44 – 01:22:38).

Nowzaradan, Jonathan and McAnally, Conor, directors. My 600-lb Life. Season 6, Episode 8, "Robert's Story." Aired February 28, 2018, on TLC. https://www.hulu.com/watch/ce27c9a8-5081-416f-bd59-dc2b17479f84.

3. Kolata, Gina, "Why Do Obese Patients Get Worst Care? Many Doctors Don't See Past the Fat," The New York Times, September 25, 2016, https://www.nytimes.com/2016/09/26/health/obese-patients-health-care.html.

Phelan, S. M., Burgess, D. J., Yeazel, M. W., Hellerstedt, W. L., Griffin, J. M., and van Ryn, M., "Impact of Weight Bias and Stigma on Quality of Care and Outcomes for Patients with Obesity," Obesity Reviews 16, no. 4, (April 2015): 319 – 326, doi: 10.1111/obr.12266.

4. Chastain, Ragen, December 15, 2017, "Helpful phrases at the doctor's office." Facebook, December 15, 2017, https://www.facebook.com/changelikethemoon/.

5. National Association of Social Workers. Code of Ethics of the National Association of Social Workers. Washington, DC: National Association of Social Workers, 2018.

CONCLUSION

CONTENT WARNING: *This chapter contains the word* ob*sity.

I would like to think of this book as just the start of many conversations to come about what it means to be a large woman and to live a full and satisfying life, even as there are *still* so many forces in the world that hold a stake in large-bodied people continuing to be self-loathing, and who believe that we are irrelevant and undeserving of basic things like dignity, respect, and joy. Yes! Joy! I hope that this book has challenged any negative perceptions that you have about yourself and that it has given you opportunities to begin to reshape your beliefs about your body. Indeed, what you believe about your body can and will have a tremendous impact on what you believe is possible for your life.

Size It Up for Yourself – Journal Entry

Let's take a moment to think about your experience as you read this book:
- What information did you find to be helpful?
- What had an immediate and direct impact on your life and on your experience in your body?
- What ideas felt challenging for you? Are you interested in exploring

> **Size It Up for Yourself – Journal Entry**
>
> *(continued)* those ideas more? If so, do you need the support of a friend or a helping professional?
> - What, if anything, was missing in this book that feels relevant to your experience as a woman living in a large body?
> - What, if anything, needs to happen for you to continue to make use of the information in this book to support you in living well?

A Changing World (Crisis = Opportunity)

I started working on the final edits to this book just as the novel coronavirus (COVID-19) pandemic began to ravage our planet. Soon after, the murder of an unarmed Black man by a police officer in Minneapolis, MN sparked weeks of mass protests worldwide that, for a minute—largely because of the response from the United States federal government and law enforcement at the ground level—appeared to be spiraling out of control. It is a scary time to be alive; a time that none of us could have imagined before March 2020. From my perspective, it feels like the Universe has imploded in the face of the injustices that have been allowed to persist for so long—environmental abuse and neglect, nationalism, xenophobia, systemic racism, classism, greed, poverty—while we, the citizens of the world, have been complacent and compliant. A boiling point has been reached and, if we are to survive, we have no choice but to ACT.

So, the time feels ripe to be thinking about and talking about and **doing something** about the injustices large people experience every day. In the same way that the pandemic has eliminated so many of the distractions that allowed this country and the world to look away from the injustices of systemic racism—leading to the national and international expansion of the BLACK LIVES MATTER movement—the floodgates will likely remain open enough for the voices and experiences of large people to be heard in a way that they have not been heard before. But only if we can find ways to make our voices louder and the pain of our experiences more visible. Unfortunately, it seems that unless enough people are made to feel uncomfortable about the plight of others, things will not change.

I am aware that it is *a lot* to ask a group of people who have found solace in their silence and safety in remaining in the shadows to intentionally make themselves seen. But as we have witnessed through other movements, there is power and safety and courage in numbers. This fight for our place in the world does not have to be fought alone. And it can be fought in ways big and small, public and private. In fact, any *tiny* step that you take to actively integrate the beliefs that are embodied in even one of the amendments of *The Large Person's Bill of Rights* into your life, is a step toward liberating yourself—and others—from the shackles of size bigotry.

The Impact of the 2020 Pandemic on the Lives of Large Women

Just as we have all been impacted by the pandemic in ways that are unique to our own life experience, so too have those of us who live in large bodies been affected. Early on, information started to circulate that suggested that large people are at a higher risk for contracting COVID-19.[1] With headlines like, "Is Being Overweight a COVID-19 Risk?" and ". . . Severe Obesity Boosts Risk of COVID-19 Death," it is no wonder that people like me are hiding out within the confines of our homes! But these headlines read like much of the information disseminated about the health of large people: they lean heavily on the assumption that if one has a "high" BMI (thirty or above), then one also has (or will have) co-occurring, chronic health conditions that the medical establishment associates with "obesity." If you take a closer look at many of the studies that *suggest* that having a large body *causes* certain chronic health conditions, you will find that almost none of them have been able to confirm that this is true. But the medical community, by and large, functions as if it is. And this often leads to biased behaviors, including providing substandard treatment because of a devaluing of the lives of people with large bodies and the uninformed judgments that are made about how we manage our health. Even if we were able to prove beyond a shadow of a doubt that there is a causal link between "obesity" and certain health conditions, and that having these health conditions puts one at greater risk for developing life-threatening complications of COVID-19, that does not mean that we, as large people, are at a greater risk for contracting the virus. Let me be clear: **There is nothing about being a large person that puts us at greater risk for contracting COVID-19.** According to the most up-to-date information that we have from the Centers for Disease Control and Prevention (CDC),

> COVID-19 spreads when an infected person breathes out droplets and very small particles that contain the virus. These droplets and particles can be breathed in by other people or land on their eyes, noses, or mouth. In some circumstances, they may contaminate surfaces they touch.[2]

Many of the headlines and broadcast news leads on the topic are meant to be provocative to capture our attention. However, they often perpetuate negative beliefs and stereotypes about the lives and experiences of people who live in large bodies.

There is a lot of work to be done to change attitudes and to improve the quality of health care for large people. But we are currently in a crisis. And a crisis calls for us to shift into survival mode. At a time when emergency responders and health care professionals are already strained by the demands of responding to this crisis, I would not want you or I to be in the position of having to wonder if we are getting the same level of care as cis-sized patients. So, please:

- Follow the guidelines for prevention and safety that are recommended by the Centers for Disease Control and Prevention.
- Plan to have virtual visits with your health care providers whenever possible.
- Feed your mind, body, and soul well; take all your medications for any chronic health conditions that you have, and get plenty of rest.

The current pandemic has also triggered an economic recession that has caused many businesses, large and small, to close their doors. I am especially saddened by the fact that some retailers of clothing for large women are closing brick-and-mortar locations, or going out of business completely. Some of them are "pivoting" to online sales, thank goodness, but this is not the same as being able to go into a store, see the displays, try clothes on, and have the full shopping experience. Our hopes for an end to this pandemic have been greatly quelled by the reality that we will likely be living with some version of it for some time. I want to encourage everyone to patronize retailers who sell goods and services that benefit large people **as much as you can**. Helping these businesses to survive is one way to ensure that our needs get met and that our community is strengthened.

With all the ways that the coronavirus (COVID-19) pandemic has negatively affected us, however, is it possible that there might also be some **silver linings** in this experience? I think so. As I mentioned earlier, this is a moment when the country feels primed to be more sensitive to injustices that have previously been overlooked. We have a rare opportunity to add our voices to the already spirited discourse on inequity. What are some of the ways that we can do this?

Another "silver lining" has been that some of my psychotherapy clients have experienced this moment as a time for reflection and renewal. Indeed, I was struck by how profoundly the Earth has regenerated herself over the past couple of years: the canals in Venice were clearing, the Himalayas were, once again, visible[3] . . . and the trees in my neighborhood were bursting with brilliant color, the likes of which I have never seen before. We can take a lesson from nature and use this time of inactivity to restore ourselves, as well. This is a perfect time to invest in ourselves, and to direct some focused time and energy on improving our experience in the world. I am so pleased to offer this book as a resource for just that.

Lovingly wishing you wellness.

FOOTNOTES

1. Caffrey, Mary, "Kaiser Study: Severe Obesity Boosts Risk of COVID-19 Death, Especially for the Young," *American Journal of Managed Care*, August 12, 2020, https://www.ajmc.com/view/kaiser-severe-obesity-boosts-risk-of-covid-19-death-especially-for-the-young.

McCallum, Katie, "Obesity & COVID-19: Can Your Weight Alone Put You at Higher Risk?," Houston Methodist (blog), accessed September 3, 2020, https://www.houstonmethodist.org/blog/articles/2020/jun/obesity-and-covid-19-can-your-weight-alone-put-you-at-higher-risk/.

"Obesity, Metabolic Syndrome Tied to Risk of COVID Infection, Severity," Center for Infectious Disease Research and Policy, University of Minnesota (website), published on August 26, 2020, https://www.cidrap.umn.edu/news-perspective/2020/08/obesity-metabolic-syndrome-tied-risk-covid-infection-severity.

Zoe Health Study. "Is Being Overweight a COVID-19 Risk?"Zoe.September 14, 2020, https://covid.joinzoe.com/us-post/covid-obesity.

Thankfully, since the original draft of this book was written, there are now vaccines and treatments available for the fight against COVID-19. However, the recommendations that I have provided above continue to be practical, relevant strategies for prevention and for your overall health and wellness.

2. U.S. Department of Health & Human Services, Centers for Disease Control and Prevention, How COVID-19 Spreads, last updated August 11, 2022, https://cdc.gov/coronavirus/2019-ncov/prevent-getting-sick/how-covid-spreads.html.

3. Kummer, Frank. "7 Ways the Planet Has Gotten Better Since the Coronavirus Shutdown." The Philadelphia Inquirer, updated April 22, 2020. https://www.inquirer.com/science/climate/earth-day-coronavirus-philadelphia-wildlife-pollution-climate-change-20200422.html

APPENDIX A

THE LARGE PERSON'S BILL OF RIGHTS

I have the right to love, accept, and appreciate my body, regardless of its size, shape, condition, or ability.

I have the right to fair and equal treatment, regardless of my size, including protection from discrimination, ridicule, bullying and harassment.

I have the right to be liked, loved, cared for, and appreciated by others, regardless of my size.

I have the right to be treated with dignity and respect, regardless of my size.

I have the right to not make self-deprecating comments or jokes, and to live free from size-related embarrassment, humiliation, and shame.

I have the right to fully engage in all of the physical, emotional, and social (including romantic love) activities of life at the size that I am now—with or without any plans to make changes to my size or weight.

I have the right to wear whatever I choose, and to adorn my body in a manner that feels good to me, regardless of what others might think.

I have the right to reasonable accommodations in public spaces, such as seating that is comfortable and supportive.

I have the right to make lifestyle changes to improve my health and well being while maintaining a loving and accepting attitude toward myself and my body as I am today, without the need to adopt an attitude of self- or body-loathing.

I have the right to make my own decisions about how I will manage my health (including my food choices). No one, including my health care providers and fitness consultants, has the right to bully me about my choices by arguing that they are concerned about my health.

I have the right to honor my body's limitations, without shame or embarrassment.

I have the right to respectfully use or take up space, and to be open and expansive in my body, and to not feel the need to cover, hide, decrease, shrink away, or otherwise attempt to appear smaller to avoid real or perceived judgment from others.

***I have the right to** quality health care from health care providers who treat me with dignity and respect, take my symptoms seriously, and engage in thorough assessment and treatment practices that are free from size-related bias.

© 2015 Leslie C. Glass
*added in 2017

APPENDIX B – WORKSHEETS

(#1) Size It Up for Yourself: Chapter Three

Journal Exercise: Challenging Negative Beliefs

Instructions:

Column 1 (negative belief): List all the negative beliefs that you are aware of having about yourself and your body.

Column 2 (origin): Now, think about where each of these beliefs originated. They might be the result of a personal experience(s) that you have had, or they might be a negative message that you have taken in from society. It might be helpful to try to remember the first time that you remember feeling this way about yourself or your body.[1] Give yourself as much time as you need to really hone in on the origin of these beliefs. This will help you in the process of ridding yourself of them.

Column 3: Are you ready to begin the process of challenging these beliefs? I will warn you: it will probably not be easy. Some of them have been burrowing their way into our nervous systems for a long time and have taken up residence. I have faith that you can do it. So, let's get started.

What evidence do you have that a belief is not true?[2]

What did you learn about this belief as a result of the work that you did in Column 2?

		NEGATIVE BELIEF
		ORIGIN
		CHALLENGE

(#2) Size It Up for Yourself: Chapter Nine
HEALTHY LIFESTYLE CHANGES PROCESS CHART

Health/Wellness CONCERN:	Barriers to Improvement:	Compassionate Solutions:	Healthy Rewards:	Process Notes:

APPENDIX C

RESOURCES FOR LARGE WOMEN

♥ = Author Recommendation

ADVOCACY

Association for Size Diversity and Health (ASDAH)
https://www.sizediversityandhealth.org
♥ *Council on Size and Weight Discrimination*
cswd.org
♥ *National Association to Advance Fat Acceptance (NAAFA)*
https://www.naafaonline.com

ACCESSIBILITY

AllGo/An Accessibility App for Plus-Size People
https://canweallgo.com
"A review app where plus-size people rate the comfort and accessibility of public spaces so others can know what to expect."

AIR TRAVEL:

North American Airlines on Rules for Overweight Passengers
https://www.tripsavvy.com/airline-rules-for-overweight-passengers-53194
♥ *Will Your Airline Make You Buy An Extra Seat On The Plane? List of Airlines' Chubby People Policies*
https://www.chubbydiaries.com/post/will-your-airline-make-you-buy-an-extra-seat-on-the-plane-list-of-airlines-chubby-people-policies

Travel:
♥ ***ChubbyDiaries.com***

Jeff Jenkins is on a mission to inspire large people to travel. His site includes tips for easing the traveling woes that come with being a large person in a not-so-size-friendly world; videos of his travels; and opportunities for group travel.

FITNESS

(PA – Philadelphia area)
♥ ***Yoga with Bliss™***
https://www.youtube.com/user/kellybliss/videos?app=desktop

"Kelly Bliss, the fat old lady who does yoga, shows you HOW to adapt the moves to meet your needs. Want to join us on Sat 10am EST? Text me for an invite. Want some phone coaching/counseling? Text me …215-303-5391!"

HEALTH
Lymphedema Support Network
https://www.lymphoedema.org

LGBTQIA+

Blogs:
Tasha Fierce
Tasha Fierce is a queer Black feminist writer.
https://tashafierce.com
This is Thin Privilege
https://thisisthinprivilege.tumblr.com

Organizations:
NOLOSE

An "organization dedicated to ending the oppression of fat people and creating vibrant fat queer culture."
nolose.org

SIZE-AFFIRMING MEDIA

FILMS:
♥ *Dumplin'*
Available on Netflix
Fattitude
www.fattitudethemovie.squarespace.com/

MAGAZINES:
FabUplus Magazine
https://fabuplusmagazine.com/
A "media landscape that celebrates health, fitness, and lifestyle for the curvy community"

MUSIC:
Beautiful, Christina Aguilera
Unpretty, TLC
Video, India.Arie

PODCASTS:
Fat, Black, and Femme
https://fatblackandfemme.blogspot.com
She's All Fat
https://shesallfatpod.com

TELEVISION SHOWS:
♥ *My Mad Fat Diary* (2013 – 2015), Available on Hulu
♥ *Shrill* (2019), Available on Hulu
♥ *This is Us* (2016), NBC, also available online

WEBSITES:
♥ Change Like the Moon Facebook group
@changelikethemoon
♥ Fattitude

SIZE-AFFIRMING THERAPISTS

NORTH CAROLINA
(Greensboro)
Three Birds Counseling, 336-430-6694
threebirdscounseling.com
threebirdscounseling@gmail.com

PENNSYLVANIA
(Philadelphia area)
♥ **Leslie Glass, LCSW**
215-399-0344
leslie@leslieglassandassoc.com
I also offer online wellness coaching for large women.

SOCIAL GROUPS

NEVADA
(Las Vegas)
Brie's Pop Up Parties
https://briespopupparties.com

NEW JERSEY
(various locations)
BABS Big and Beautiful
babsbbw.com/
Hosts parties and social networking events that are primarily attended by Black/African American folks. Also hosts an annual multi-day event called Summer Jam.

NATIONAL
Nationwide BBW Club Calendar Facebook group
Find a plus-size friendly event in your area.

GLOSSARY

BBW. An abbreviation for Big Beautiful Woman/Women, a term that is frequently used as a positive way of describing large women. The original use of the term is credited to Carol Shaw, the founder of *BBW Magazine* (c. 1979), a fashion and lifestyle magazine for large women;[1] however, the term has since become a part of pop culture. Please be aware that the abbreviation has also frequently been used in the titles of pornographic material that features large women, so you will likely encounter some of that material if you use "BBW" as an Internet search term on its own.

Bashes. The name that is frequently given to parties that are held worldwide for women and men who identify as BBW/BHM (Big Handsome Men), SSBBW/SSBHM (Super-sized Big Handsome Men) "and their admirers." I intentionally used quotation marks for the preceding phrase because, although it is often used to describe these parties, it has a bit of the flavor of marginalizing large people (i.e. "admirers" has the connotation of people who fetishize large women, which feels immediately objectifying to me). What are your thoughts?

Body Mass Index (BMI). CONTENT WARNING: *This definition contains the word* ob*sity. A person's weight in kilograms divided by the square of their height in meters (Centers for Disease Control and Prevention 2020). This calculation is frequently used by physicians as a predictor of health problems that are believed to be associated with "obesity."

It is believed that, the higher a person's BMI (according to the CDC, the "normal or healthy" range for women is 18.5–24.9), the greater their risk is for developing health problems that are associated with "obesity."

Cis-sized. As I stated in the preface, I use this term to refer to everyone who is not in the range of sizes that are typically thought of as large. "Cis-" is a Latin prefix that means "on this side of" (Steinmetz 2014)—in this case, cis-sized people are on the side of what has been deemed socially acceptable.

Cis-sized normativity. The belief that it is "normal" for bodies to be within the range of sizes that go roughly from size zero to size twelve (for women), and that anyone who wears a size that is larger than size ten is considered outside of the norm. This belief is articulated when people and/or systems expect people with large bodies to lose enough weight to be within an "acceptable" range of sizes; or to adapt or conform in situations that do not meet their size-related needs (e.g., the absence of supportive, comfortable, and accessible seating).

Microaggression. The Merriam-Webster Dictionary defines a microaggression as "a comment or action that subtly and often unconsciously or unintentionally expresses a prejudiced attitude toward a member of a marginalized group (such as a racial minority)."

Self-determination. "An ethical principle in social work which recognizes the rights and needs of clients to be free to make their own choices and decisions."[2]

Super-sized. A term that is used by some to refer to women who are 400 or more pounds. It is often combined with BBW (as in SSBBW).

"SSBBW," Urban Dictionary, July 21, 2006, https://www.urbandictionary.com/define.php?term=SSBBW.

ABOUT THE AUTHOR

Leslie C. Glass is a licensed clinical social worker (LCSW) and couples and family therapist (MFT) with twenty-six years of experience working in the mental health field. Since 2007, she has owned and operated a private psychotherapy practice in Philadelphia, PA, specializing in providing therapeutic support for the LGBTQ+ and ethnic minority communities, and in the treatment of trauma-related disorders. She is also currently building a niche and specialty around clinical work with women who live in large bodies.